HOME DESIGN WORKBOOKS

# STUDIO
# LIVING

# HOME DESIGN WORKBOOKS
# STUDIO
# LIVING

## SYLVIA KATZ

**DORLING KINDERSLEY**
LONDON • NEW YORK • SYDNEY • MOSCOW

## A DORLING KINDERSLEY BOOK

**Project Editor** IRENE LYFORD
**Project Art Editor** INA STRADINS
**DTP Designer** MARK BRACEY
**Location Photography** JAKE FITZJONES
**Studio Photography** ANDY CRAWFORD, MATTHEW WARD
**Stylist** SHANI ZION
**Production Controller** MICHELLE THOMAS
**Series Editor** CHARLOTTE DAVIES
**Series Art Editor** CLIVE HAYBALL

First published in Great Britain in 1997 by
Dorling Kindersley Limited
9 Henrietta Street, London WC2E 8PS

A CIP catalogue record for this book
is available from the British Library

ISBN 0 7513 04700

Text film output in Great Britain by The Right Type
Reproduced in Singapore by Pica
Printed and bound in Great Britain by Butler & Tanner Ltd
at Frome and London

# INTRODUCTION • 6

# STUDIO LIVING ELEMENTS • 18

## ROOM PLANS • 48

## PLOT YOUR DESIGN • 74

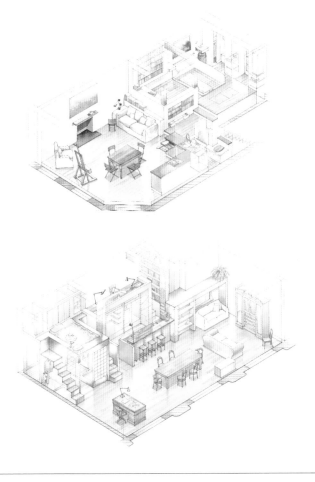

CONTENTS

# INTRODUCTION

△ **SHIPSHAPE KITCHEN**
The galley of a motor yacht illustrates how to pack a complete mini kitchen, with sink, oven, microwave and hob, into a tiny space.

L IVING IN ONE ROOM can be hell. But it can also be fun if you are prepared to be adventurous with space and furniture. Of course "one room" can describe many different shapes and sizes, from a tiny "bedsit" to a galleried, open-plan apartment. However, the basics remain the same, and it is what you do with them that counts.

For many reasons, both social and cultural, family units are growing smaller and this, in turn, has created a rising demand for one-room apartments. Couples without children, single professional people, those wanting a city *pied-à-terre*, and separated or divorced people are among the large group of mainly city-dwellers for whom one-room living has become either a choice or a necessity.

Living in one space certainly has economic advantages, such as lower rent, heating, and lighting costs, but it also has enormous creative

**SLEEPING CAPSULES** ▷
The Japanese, familiar with cramped, multi-functional living spaces, devised the capsule hotel as a one-night stop for travellers prepared to put basic amenities above luxury and space.

potential and it can challenge you to think very clearly about yourself and your lifestyle and to crystallize aspects of your personality and your way of doing things. These will determine the layout of your living space and the furniture and fittings that will make it work for you.

## SOURCES OF INSPIRATION

Most of us have experienced life in a confined space, such as a tent, caravan, or boat, and have enjoyed it tremendously. What the experience teaches you is the importance of organization, how to reduce your needs to essentials, and how to simplify and streamline your actions. You also learn, through improvisation, how to adapt what you have for other purposes. In the same way, one-room living concentrates the mind and challenges your ingenuity and imagination – there is no room for superfluous baggage.

The inspiration for many of the ideas in this book can be traced to houseboats and barges, Pullman carriages, and cruise ships. Today's motorized homes are fitted with sophisticated furnishings that cleverly combine living room, kitchen, dining room, bathroom, and bedroom. When you think about it – and once you have discarded traditional notions of what you actually need in order to live comfortably – you realize that all the necessities for everyday life can be fitted into a few cupboards. A wall of fitted cupboards, containing kitchen, wardrobe and bed (*see opposite*) has just been incorporated into a London mews flat, but many other elegant solutions to one-room living have been inspired by the Japanese approach to life in a minimal,

multi-functional space. Sliding, translucent screens provide a flexible way of dividing living areas, while taking up very little space. The futon has been accepted in the West as a simple sofa-bed (although in Japan a futon, without a base, is rolled up and stored during the day). The capsule hotel may not be to everybody's taste, but it does illustrate how to reduce sleeping accommodation to its most expedient level.

Technological changes in the workplace are another major influence on our living patterns. Innovations such as laptops, modems, and mobile phones, and the introduction of flexible working practices, have liberated us from a fixed workplace, and are blurring the boundaries between home and office, work and leisure.

All of these changes are reflected in a growing market for adaptable, multi-purpose, space-saving products, and manufacturers and designers have begun to tailor their designs to satisfy this new demand. Tapering baths, swivelling handbasins, and corner options on everything from showers and sinks to storage units; these are just some of the new product species that are emerging in response to the demands of our new way of living.

In this book we have included some of the best examples of such products and designs to stimulate your search for ways of making the most of a limited living space.

△ **FOLD-AWAY LIVING**
Most of the essentials of one-room living can be fitted into a few cupboards. This wall, finished in Italian-style plaster, hides a fold-out kitchen, a fold-down bed, and a fold-out wardrobe. The doors of the kitchen and the wardrobe contain built-in storage.

INDUSTRIAL SPACE ▽
The conversion of obsolete industrial buildings has created a new type of living space, with exposed beams and brickwork and double height ceiling that allows for the construction of a gallery level and suspended storage.

## EVALUATE YOUR ROOM

Examine your room objectively, picking out positive features that can be developed, and noting the weaker areas that need improvement.
☐ Are there spaces such as alcoves and chimney breasts or understair areas with potential for built-in shelving and cupboards?
☐ Is there room for a permanent sleeping area, or enough ceiling height to consider constructing a raised sleeping platform?
☐ How much sunshine and natural light does the room receive during the day? Which areas of your room benefit most from these?
☐ Would it be possible to enlarge the main window to full floor-to-ceiling height, or to extend it into a balcony or patio area?
☐ Can more windows be let into an external wall if necessary?
☐ Does your room have access to a garden, roof terrace, or patio? If not, are there ledges suitable for window boxes?

Whether your prospective living space is one room in a large, converted house, a flat with two or three tiny rooms, whose dividing walls can be knocked down to create one large space, or a spacious loft apartment in a converted industrial property, your first priority in planning how to use the space is to look carefully at your future home. Study its architectural features, noting the position of all plumbing, electrical, and gas supplies, the way light enters the building, and which window offers the best view. Try to work with the existing structure and services, not against them, and a plan will begin to take shape. Basic services can, of course, be moved if necessary, and remote pumping and macerator systems are available that allow you to fit a bathroom or kitchen into a location that conventional plumbing cannot reach.

Consider your heating options, too, at planning stage: radiators, a hot air system, or even underfloor heating – a Roman invention that is currently enjoying a revival. Think, too, about any structural changes that you might want to make, such as demolishing walls,

## STARTING FROM SCRATCH

If you have the opportunity of starting from scratch, your apartment will be purpose-designed and unique to you. The "shell and core" method of loft conversion offers plumbed and wired living spaces ready to be personalized in this way.

**❶ A BLANK CANVAS**
Plumbing, drainage, and electrics are installed in the shell. Brickwork has been cleaned and ceilings plastered.

**❷ PLANNING AND BUILDING**
Living zones are planned and built on different levels using a variety of solid and translucent materials.

**❸ A PERSONALIZED SPACE**
The final loft space has living and working areas at varying heights, each contained and colour-defined.

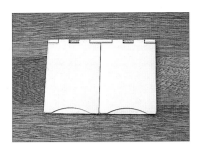

◁ **FLOOR SOCKETS**
A below-floor power circuit with flush-fitting, floor-mounted sockets provides flexibility in an open space, allowing lights, computers, and audio equipment to be moved around easily.

building a glazed extension, or enlarging or creating windows and doors. For this type of work, you will need to consult an architect who will deal with planning regulations, and help you to draw up plans and select materials.

Although overall size will influence what is possible, all one-room living spaces have certain requirements and problems in common. These centre on the basic functions of living – cooking, eating, sleeping, washing, working, and relaxing – and these areas and their requirements have been covered in detail in this book. To help focus your ideas, work through our questionnaire *Assess Your Needs* (*see pp.16–17*).

## LIVING IN LOFTS

Later in the book, we show examples of different studios and the ingenious ways in which their owners have adapted them to their needs. We

include a number of the loft apartments that are currently so fashionable. Lofts originated in New York in the 1980s, when abandoned warehouses were discovered to have valuable residential potential. The loft movement's mission to salvage disused industrial buildings that might otherwise have been demolished, retaining as far as possible the original features and industrial dimensions, has been welcomed for helping to revitalize run-down inner-city areas.

In this book you will find exciting loft spaces as small as 80 square metres (861 square feet), in which the architect has succeeded in combining the living elements essential for a decent quality of life by employing all the tricks he knows for making small spaces appear larger: raised sleeping or work platforms, curved false walls, glass bricks, full-height and full-width mirrors, and frosted glass panels, to name just a few.

Today's designers are also rediscovering age-old furniture forms to suit current lifestyles. Folding, stacking, nesting, hinged, pack-away, and clip-together units can be assembled according to individual needs, and updated versions of old favourites, such as nesting tables, are appearing.

All these devices are invaluable when planning and furnishing a very limited space. A bed or work area on a raised platform releases useful floor space, as well as offering the chance of filling the area below with storage. If you seldom need a dining table, why not store a folded table and a set of trestles out of sight? And, if ceiling height permits, create vital long-term storage space by building a false ceiling to make an "attic", or a raised floor level to form a "cellar".

△ **USING BORROWED SPACE**
Lateral thinking can solve tricky problems. Here, a washing machine has been fitted into a tiny toilet area by utilizing "dead" space from the kitchen on the other side of the wall.

△ **"HOT SPRINGS"**
Radiators come in all shapes and sizes. This wall-mounted vertical model will fit into a corner or alongside a window.

## ABOUT YOU

Before designing your space, you must ask yourself some searching questions: your answers could determine certain choices you have to make *(see p.11)*.

☐ Are you basically an untidy person? Do you have a good storage system, yet have difficulty using it? Are you uncomfortable in a tidy environment?

☐ Are you a workaholic? Do you put your work before leisure, or even before cooking? Do you own a lot of electronic equipment, a library, or a vast amount of files?

☐ Do you entertain often? Is a good deal of your time reserved for cooking, dining, and socializing with friends and family?

☐ Are you a home-maker? Do you prefer to make things yourself rather than buying them in the shops?

☐ Do you have hobbies with special equipment that your living space has to accommodate, such as a workbench, or storage space for a surfboard or skiis?

# DIVIDING AND DEFINING SPACE

Both physical and visual barriers can be used to separate different areas in a single, open-plan living space: half-height walls, translucent materials, varying floor levels, screens, and mobile shelving units – all of these can be employed in imaginative ways.

❶ TRANSLUCENT FABRICS

❷ BAMBOO ROLLER BLINDS

❸ ALUMINIUM VENETIAN BLIND

❹ RAISED PLATFORM AREA

❺ VARYING FLOOR FINISHES

❻ TOWEL RAIL/ROOM DIVIDER

❼ DIFFERENT FLOOR LEVELS

❽ HALF-HEIGHT WALLS

❾ DOUBLE-SIDED SHELVING

◁ PRIVATE SCREENING
A screen can create instant privacy. This one, made of maple veneer panels with translucent, polypropylene hinges, appears to balance with no visible fixings.

One of the fundamental questions you must ask yourself when considering the idea of living in a one-room space is how to deal with the reality of having every aspect of your living arrangements exposed, either within earshot or within view, at all times: having to share the space for living, cooking, working, sleeping, and entertaining. Your solution will depend very much on the type of person you are, so before you start planning your layout you will have to ask yourself some very personal questions and answer them as truthfully as possible. Otherwise your scheme will backfire on you (*see* "About You" *left* ).

Do you need to screen off certain areas for privacy or for peace and quiet, or would you enjoy an open-plan room? Depending on your attitude to these two central questions, you have a choice of dividing up your space in either visual or physical ways. Effective visual barriers can be remarkably simple: a change of flooring finish from carpet to tiles, a switch in flooring colour, a raised step to another floor level, or simply a large plant in a strategically placed pot. There are also ways of creating visual – but not solid – barriers for privacy, such as draped translucent fabrics, open, double-sided shelving, or vertical towel rails. Equally, there are ways of creating solid barriers, perhaps for soundproofing purposes, without them being permanent, such as sliding partitions, screens, or units on castors.

Planning and storage are the keys to one-room survival, and this applies particularly to rooms that have to double as home work spaces. Once you have discarded unnecessary furniture and belongings, look for a modular storage system that suits your lifestyle, the nature of your work, and your personality. There has been a tremendous growth in well-designed storage systems, ranging from modular stacking boxes and baskets to industrial fibreboard containers on castors. Many of the high-tech storage containers available have been inspired by the extremely functional products that are to be found in industrial and catering equipment trade catalogues.

For those who like to keep in touch with nature and have difficulty in settling for a window-box-sized garden, plants offer another way of dividing one living area from another, as well as adding a hint of nature to an urban setting. A traditional jardinière (an ornamental plant stand) can act as a low-level divider, while trailing plants on a high-level shelf soon extend downwards to become a natural wall of foliage. Among the new designs available is the plant holder shown (right), which consists of a suspended, vertical series of pop-together, transparent plastic bags, each with its own mini supply of water. This system can also be used as a decorative infill between areas of your living space – but for plants to flourish you must place it close to a good source of natural light.

HANGING GARDEN △
Clear plastic pockets and water sacs provide both an unorthodox indoor garden and an attractive vertical wall decoration, especially if the plants or herbs develop into a cascade of foliage.

BORROWED LIGHT ▽
One of the disadvantages
of building a gallery in a
converted loft is that there
may be areas with little
natural light. The use of
sandblasted glass panels in
this raised work area is one
way of allowing light to
reach those dark corners.

We take light for granted, yet it is a valuable tool for changing the shape, colour, and dimensions of an interior space. It influences the entire atmosphere of a place and our own feelings as occupants. Take every opportunity to maximize the available natural light and experiment with ways of using it to create a sense of spaciousness.

Light can be reflected around a room through the use of pale-coloured paintwork and reflective surfaces such as mirror, glass, laminate, and aluminium slatted blinds. Light can also be transmitted into the darker parts of an interior through clear and frosted glass, glass bricks, translucent paper, fabrics, and blinds. Recessed downlighters can create pools of light that act as focal points, and spotlights can be arranged to draw the eye in a certain direction, thereby creating a feeling of space.

## MANIPULATING SPACE

An external wall, or a roof that has been exposed by removing a ceiling, provides the possibility of creating another window or a skylight, or an existing window can be enlarged to increase the amount of natural light available. If you have no opportunity of doing this, create the illusion of a window by inserting a strip of wall mirror between doors or cupboards. In a similar way, a framed, wall-hung mirror can convey an effective impression of an adjoining room.

You can also manipulate space through the use of a variety of light fittings, and by the clever use of colour and pattern. For example, some colours seem to recede while others advance: dark paint will appear to lower a ceiling and bring it nearer,

△ MIRROR IMAGES
Filling a narrow wall space with a strip of mirror is an effective way of creating the illusion of a small window. The mirror will reflect any available light.

while a light, pale colour will make it recede.

When confronted with limited space, try to apply the motto of the king of modernism, the architect Mies van der Rohe: "Less is more", and cut back on clutter. But sparseness need not be cold. An overall, light colour scheme in a minimalist-style interior creates a feeling of airy space, but the hard edges can be softened with warm wooden floors, carefully selected personal objects, bright acid colours, and plants. Salvaged items and recycled materials, such as reclaimed wood and multi-coloured plastic sheet, can be sympathetic in a home environment, and are particularly valid at a time when we cannot afford to waste materials.

Today there is more need than ever to personalize your own space. Be bold, and go for what you have always wanted. You are expressing your personality and lifestyle and, after all, you are the one who must live there.

# CREATING LIGHT AND SPACE

Light is particularly important in a small or one-room living space. It can be manipulated to change the feel and shape of a room, through the use of light fittings, mirror, and glass, and by a careful choice of surface finishes and colours.

❶ ILLUMINATED GLAZED INFILL

❷ GLASS BLOCK WALL

❸ SANDBLASTED GLASS PANEL

❹ "ROOM" IN A MIRROR

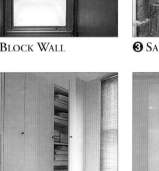

❺ MIRROR-DOUBLED SPACE

❻ REFLECTED LIGHT

❼ SHIMMERING METAL BLINDS

❽ WINDOW-LEDGE GARDEN

❾ PATIO KITCHEN EXTENSION

# HOW THIS BOOK WORKS

THIS BOOK will help you to plan a brand new studio or to adapt an existing one by giving you the practical know-how you need to design a room that matches your lifestyle and to create an efficient and comfortable living space. A series of questions helps you to assess what you want from your studio, then a survey of furniture and fittings guides you to elements that best suit those needs. Next, three-dimensional plans of six studios explain how successful designs have been engineered, and, finally, instructions on measuring and drawing up a studio plan leave you equipped to translate your own ideas into reality.

## 2. SELECT FITTINGS ▽

To help you compile a list of the features that will best suit your needs, a range of furniture and fittings are surveyed (*pp.18–47*). A "Remember" box draws your attention to the key design points, and the pros and cons of each element are discussed. Simple diagrams indicate ideal heights for kitchen worktops, work equipment, and different kinds of storage, along with advice on moving furniture and working practices.

## 1. ASSESS YOUR NEEDS ▽

Preliminary questions (*pp.16–17*) are asked to encourage you to think about your needs and the condition and potential of your present living space. By examining aspects of your lifestyle, such as how you work, relax, and entertain, you will find it easier to identify the most suitable design solutions for remodelling your studio or creating a new one.

## 4. DESIGNING YOUR STUDIO △

When you feel satisfied with your ideas for a studio, turn to *Plot Your Design* (*pp.76–81*) and put your thoughts into practice. This section provides a step-by-step guide to measuring the whole area, plus detailed instructions on how to draw up a floor plan and wall elevations to scale. Common design mistakes are pinpointed and successful solutions are shown. Arriving at a satisfactory layout takes time, so draw up variations on tracing paper and pick out the best elements from each for your final plan.

## 3. LEARN HOW TO PLAN △

A chapter on *Room Plans* (*pp.48–73*) looks in detail at six existing studio designs – including loft-style apartments in converted commercial properties – and offers advice and inspiration on how to bring together all the elements in your own plan. A three-dimensional drawing, a bird's-eye view plan, photographs, and a list of design points explain the thinking behind each design solution, while detailed annotation picks out the most interesting and relevant features.

## HOW TO USE THE GRAPH PAPER

■ Draw up your room to scale (*see pp.76–81*), using the graph paper provided (*pp.89–96*). You may photocopy if you need more.

■ For a small-scale studio, use the graph paper with a metric scale of 1:20, where one large square represents 1m and one small square represents 10cm. Therefore, an area 60cm long is drawn as six small squares. Alternatively, use the imperial scale of 1:24, where one large square represents 1ft and a small square 3in.

■ For a room with larger dimensions, use the graph paper with the smaller scale of 1:50. Again, the large squares represent 1m and the small squares 10cm. Alternatively, use the imperial graph paper with the scale of 1:48, where a large square equals 4ft and a small square 6in.

■ Having plotted your room on graph paper, start experimenting with varying designs on overlays of tracing paper.

# ASSESS YOUR NEEDS

THE FOLLOWING questions will prompt you to consider your lifestyle and needs, area by area, so that as you work through the book you will be able to identify the elements, plans, and style choices that suit you best.

## LIVING

The quality and comfort of life in a one-room interior depends on how much space you can create and how well adapted it is to your lifestyle.

□ Do you find it easiest to relax in a small intimate area, or do you like the sense of freedom found in a large open space?
□ Would you prefer to define different areas by varying the floor coverings and wall colours, or do you want to maintain a unified, open-plan space?
□ Can you arrange your living space to make the most of natural light?
□ If your space is limited, do you want to keep it uncluttered by using furniture that can be moved aside when it is not needed?
□ When you have friends to visit, are they happy to relax on floor cushions, or would they prefer more conventional seating?
□ If you have a large collection of books, can they be stored in high-level shelving in spaces that would otherwise be wasted?
□ Do you have collections of objects that you wish to display? If so, can they be housed in alcoves or wall units, or would a mobile storage unit be more useful?
□ Would a mini or portable audio unit be adequate for your needs, or do you have a system that needs special installation?
□ Would different kinds of lighting for relaxing, reading, or working improve your enjoyment of these activities?
□ How important is a garden to you? Would a window-box or indoor plant display provide a replacement?

## COOKING AND EATING

The most important influence on the design of this area is whether you see cooking and eating as important activities or as transient necessities.

□ Would you like to separate the kitchen in some way, or would you rather include it in the general living space?
□ When you are working in the kitchen, would you like to face into the living area, or would you prefer an outside view?
□ Would you like to close off the kitchen, or would you rather make a feature of it by displaying attractive equipment?
□ Are you a convenience cook, who needs only a microwave oven and fridge, or do you need space and equipment to prepare adventurous meals for yourself and guests?
□ Do you use some pieces of equipment more frequently than others? Can they be stored so that they are accessible, with heavy equipment stored at low levels?
□ Do you like to sit down at a table for everyday meals, or are you happy with a more informal tray or breakfast bar?
□ Would you like a dining table that can be extended when necessary, or could you manage with a folding or trestle table that can be put away when not in use?
□ If space is limited, would a slimline or table-top dishwasher fit? Do you really need such equipment?

□ If you spend a lot of time in the kitchen area, are you sure that the flooring is durable but "giving" and easy to clean?
□ Is your cooking area in an unventilated or tight space? Have you considered an extractor fan or waste disposal unit?

## WORKING

The design of your work area depends on whether you are happy working on the kitchen table, or whether you need privacy and a businesslike atmosphere.

□ If you work from home, do you need a dedicated work space, or would a surface that can be folded away or double as a dining table suffice?
□ Have you taken into account your realistic day-to-day and long-term work storage needs? Can you plan in sufficient file and shelf space near your work area for easy retrieval?
□ Does your work require much specialist equipment? Can you arrange your work space so that there is access to ample power and telephone points?
□ Would a purpose-built mobile computer table with shelves for printer and keyboard best suit your needs?
□ Is good natural light or task lighting essential for your work?
□ Can you concentrate easily or do you need some sort of barrier, such as screens or a room divider, to prevent distraction?
□ Can you adjust your work furniture and equipment in order to achieve maximum comfort and efficiency?
□ Do you want your work area to look like an office, or would you prefer it to blend in to your interior scheme?
□ Would screening your work area give a more professional impression when clients visit you?
□ Is it important to you that your household accounts are well organized and accessible?

# WASHING

Your bathing habits will determine the siting and design of your bathroom. With imaginative planning, a bath can be installed even in restricted spaces.

☐ Which do you prefer: a shower or a bath? If space is limited, would you consider devoting the entire space to a luxury shower-room, or could you install a space-saving bath?

☐ Do you need a separate bathroom or could you incorporate a bath or shower cubicle into your living area?

☐ Can you make use of space above the bath and WC for bathroom storage? Do you have enough shelves and cabinets for toiletries so that the basin area does not become too cluttered?

☐ If your bathroom is likely to be used by visitors, have you considered how much of the contents you might prefer to conceal?

☐ Do you have the space for a large cupboard for spare towels, or will they have to be stored elsewhere?

☐ Have you made provision for clothes, such as hooks for bathrobes, a laundry hamper, and a bathroom chair?

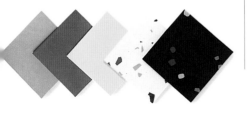

# SLEEPING AND DRESSING

Would you feel happier with a semi-private, defined "bedroom" area, or must the bed double as seating during the daytime, and the sleeping area be used for working and relaxing?

☐ Can you be bothered with the inconvenience of a foldaway bed, or one that doubles as seating during the day, or would you prefer a permanent bed, either on the floor or on a raised platform?

☐ Is privacy in your sleeping area important? Would curtains provide adequate screening, or would you prefer something more substantial?

☐ What do you like to keep by your bed? Have you provided for storage of your alarm clock, reading material, and so on?

☐ If you plan to erect a platform bed, is there a source of natural light and ventilation nearby?

☐ How much hanging, shelf, and drawer space do you need for clothes? How do you like to store out-of-season clothing?

☐ Would you like a dressing area with a full-length mirror and good lighting?

☐ Are you likely to have guests to stay? Do you have room to store a foldaway bed, or could you have seating that doubles as a bed, such as a futon, sofa-bed, studio couch, or truckle bed?

# UTILITIES

In the early stages of planning, allocate spaces for cleaning-equipment storage and for clothes drying, as well as for plumbing in a washing machine.

☐ Will you need facilities to do your own laundry, or do you send it out?

☐ If space is limited would a half-size or table-top washing machine suit you?

☐ Will you need to install a clothes drying rack or pulley, or do you have a drier?

☐ Have you planned for a ventilated cupboard for storing bulky cleaning equipment, such as vacuum cleaners?

☐ Could you have a space-saving fold-out ironing table fitted into a kitchen unit, or do you have room for a full-size model?

# STORAGE

A good storage system is an absolute necessity for studio living in order to reduce clutter and keep belongings in some degree of order.

☐ Do you prefer to hide clutter behind doors, or do you like the idea of using open containers, such as baskets and hanging wall pockets?

☐ Will you need space for long-term storage, such as gardening and sports equipment, tools, and DIY material?

☐ If you don't want a fitted appearance in your kitchen, can you adapt existing pieces of furniture for storage?

☐ Do you have equipment that requires storage at a controlled temperature?

☐ Will items in long-term storage need protection from dust and insects?

☐ If you have valuables, is it worth investing in a safe for security?

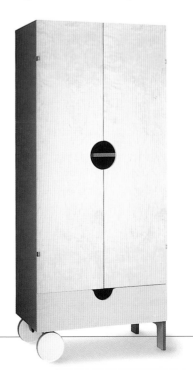

STUDIO LIVING ELEMENTS

# LIVING AREA

WHEN SPACE IS LIMITED, multi-functional furniture is the most practical choice. Look for sofas that convert to beds and for folding and stacking chairs that can be hung on the wall or stored in a corner when not in use. Nesting tables are intrinsically space saving, while portable pieces are extremely versatile. Make use of any spaces inside and under seating by packing with storage containers.

## FLEXIBLE SEATING

Two types of seating are particularly well suited to one-room living: modular pieces provide maximum flexibility and function, as well as comfort, whereas minimal seating, which can be folded up or stacked when not in use, is ideal for maximizing the use of limited space.

*INTERLOCKING PIECES*
*The sections of this fabric-covered foam seating system also fit together to form a block that can be laid horizontally, to provide an occasional double bed, or arranged vertically, to form a sculptural screen.*

*SIMPLE CONSTRUCTION*
*Polyurethane foam is cut to shape and covered in stretch jersey fabric.*

*CONVERSATION PIECES*
*Modular seating allows for the separate pieces to be arranged to meet the demands of any social occasion.*

**FOLDING CHAIR △**
An up-to-date version of an old favourite, this brushed aluminium chair with canvas seat and back is comfortable, lightweight, and easily stored when not in use.

**MODULAR SEATING △**
Designed originally in the 1960s, these fabric-covered foam shapes are both practical and fun. As well as offering endless seating permutations to suit a variety of lifestyles and interiors, they can double as a spare bed (*see above*).

**CONVERTIBLE SEATING ▷**
Sofas that convert to beds are available in many shapes and sizes, including the traditional folding version with integral mattress, and futons on folding bases. Shown here is a studio couch that opens sideways to become a single bed.

# ADAPTABLE TABLES

While there is always a need for small side tables, in restricted living spaces the emphasis must be on adaptable units that not only provide convenient surfaces but also double as stools or storage units. Look for designs that offer extra flexibility, such as nesting and folding tables, or units on castors that can be moved easily from one part of the room to another as required.

△ NESTING TABLES AND CHEST
Space-saving nesting tables are widely available. This imaginative Italian design has extended the idea to include a small chest of drawers.

**VARIABLE HEIGHT**
*Simple adjustable vertical supports increase the usefulness of this small table.*

◁ **ADJUSTABLE TABLE**
With a base that is large enough to provide stability in all positions, a simple height-adjustable table can be used as a small dining-table or plant stand.

△ SPACE-SAVING SEATING
When not in use this ingenious version of the truckle bed slides under the low-level platform unit – which serves as a seating area – leaving the spaciousness of the interior undiminished.

**WALL-HUNG TABLE/PICTURE** ▷
This unusual design, made in beech, steel, and glass, offers more than a side table: a picture or photograph of your choice can be displayed beneath the clipped-on glass top so that when the table is folded up it can be hung on the wall as a work of art.

**VERSATILITY**
*Both the top and the base of this table fold flat for wall-hanging.*

△ OPEN TABLE          △ FOLDED TABLE

**BEECH FRAMEWORK**
*The main structure of the unit is made from polished beech-veneered plywood.*

**ALUMINIUM ADDITIONS**
*Sheet aluminium has been cut and folded to form the drawers and legs.*

**TABLE-CHEST** ▽
Look for multi-purpose designs, such as this beautifully made, beech-veneered table-chest. The clever use of hinges allows for easy adaptation from space-saving chest of drawers to low table, without disturbing the contents of the two aluminium drawers.

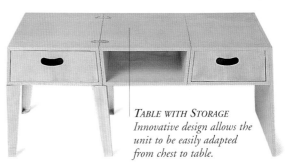

**TABLE WITH STORAGE**
*Innovative design allows the unit to be easily adapted from chest to table.*

# STORAGE AND DISPLAY

Flexible storage is vital for maintaining a sense of uncluttered space in a studio or loft. Fixed, free-standing cabinets take up space, but mobile pieces can be moved around to suit different occasions. Think laterally and discover unexpected places for fitting shelves and cupboards, such as the doorway between one room and another, where a false passage filled with shelving can be created. Glass shelving provides an attractive method of displaying favourite objects and collections, without interrupting the surrounding flow of light and space.

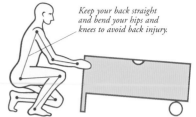

## CORRECT LIFTING

*Keep your back straight and bend your hips and knees to avoid back injury.*

When lifting heavy objects, keep your back straight and bend your knees, then slowly straighten into the upright position.

### REMEMBER

■ Assess every corner space for its storage potential. Even very narrow gaps can be fitted with small shelves for CDs, or used to store sports equipment.

■ Fit furniture with castors so that you can easily alter the interior layout. Bookshelves can be moved to provide an instant screen, while storage chests can double as tables.

■ Make the most of walls and ceilings for storage purposes, thus freeing limited floor space.

### COLOURFUL CUBE ▽
Based on the fridge-door concept, the interlocking door of this cabinet forms part of the storage space. The unit is mounted on five castors, one of which is on the door.

*MOBILE STORAGE*
*Providing an attractive display cabinet when open, this mobile unit doubles as a side table.*

△ NO WASTED SPACE
With a variety of cupboards and shelves, this wall is entirely filled with storage, while the doorway to the adjoining room has been converted into a passage with shelving. White paintwork gives a light and spacious feeling to this intensively used space.

*DOUBLE-SIDED STORAGE*
*With sections large enough to hold a mini sound system or stacks of boxes, this unit is a versatile piece of furniture.*

### STORAGE DIVIDER ▷
Measuring 173cm (68in) high by 163cm (64in) wide, this beech-veneered storage unit on locking steel wheels can act as both a temporary room divider and as a multi-purpose storage unit with access from both sides.

**PRACTICAL PORTABILITY △**
Wheels turn this colourful box, with its birch-veneered lid, into a versatile trolley to provide a storage bench with a multi-purpose surface that can be moved around as required.

# AUDIO-VISUAL ENTERTAINMENT

In a small space, the storage of audio-visual equipment calls for ingenious solutions. Wall brackets, designed for televisions and loudspeakers, free valuable floor space, while mobile television and video trolleys allow the equipment to be wheeled out of sight when not in use.

**△ STORAGE AS SCULPTURE**
Among the wide and imaginative range of CD racks now available, from free-standing towers to slot-together systems, this simple and elegant model in natural wood turns CD storage into a wall-mounted work of art.

**ALL-ROUND VIEWING △**
This well-made, wall-mounted steel and alloy television support, with secure fixings, has a tilt and swivel action that allows the set to be viewed from any angle.

*SWIVELLING SHELF*
*The swivelling top section increases the versatility of this television and video trolley.*

*DOUBLE-SIDED*
*Accessible from both sides, the shelf spaces of this unit can be used for CD or video storage.*

**△ MOBILE TELEVISION TROLLEY**
Mobile pieces of furniture, such as this solid beech storage unit, are particularly useful in restricted living spaces, where it is often convenient to move items out of the way when they are not being used. This unit, although designed for television or sound-system storage, could equally well be used for work storage or as a handy bedside cabinet. The unit is mounted on rubber-tyred castors for easy movement.

# Cooking Area

Caravans and boats provide excellent examples of the super-organization and streamlined, logical planning that are the key to successful cooking in a small space. The first step is to take account of how you shop and cook, so that you can make informed decisions about what equipment you need.

## Cookers and Fresh-food Storage

Limit yourself to two rings or burners – unless you honestly think that you need more – and opt instead for cooking methods that are both space- and energy-saving, such as multi-tiered pans, slow cookers, and microwave ovens. However little cooking you do, you will need storage for perishable food. Fridges come in all sizes and styles, including table-top and slimline models.

△ Triple Saucepan Set
Cook a complete meal on one ring in this classic three-part saucepan – an economy that is as relevant today as when the set was first designed.

△ Multi-tiered Cooking
Based on the Indian and Chinese method of stacking containers over one heat source, this is a supremely efficient cooking system.

Complete Kitchen ▷
As a ready-assembled unit, this self-contained mini kitchen is ready to be fitted and connected to power sources and plumbing. It provides a neat solution to food preparation in a very restricted space.

*Heavy Doors*
*Each of the extra-wide doors is hung on four hinges and reinforced down the hinge side.*

*Kitchen Sink*
*Neatly incorporated into the unit are a small sink, drainer, and two hot plates.*

*Hidden Kitchen*
*Two large doors, each lined with shelves from top to bottom, open out to reveal a self-contained, fully fitted kitchen.*

*Built-in Microwave Oven*
*The inclusion of a microwave oven is a boon to those with busy lifestyles, and extends the range of cooking options.*

*Full-size Fridge*
*Although the whole unit measures only 1000 x 600 x 900mm (39 x 23 x 35in), refrigerator capacity is not reduced.*

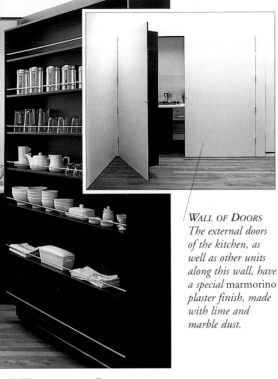

△ KITCHEN IN A CUPBOARD
The generous dimensions of this elegant cupboard kitchen provide ample storage space for china and non-perishable supplies on the shelves that line the inner surface of the doors. Downward-flowing light from a narrow glazed roof light illuminates the kitchen worktop.

*WALL OF DOORS*
*The external doors of the kitchen, as well as other units along this wall, have a special* marmorino *plaster finish, made with lime and marble dust.*

MOBILE WORKSURFACE ▷
A mobile food preparation surface, such as this maplewood trolley, is very useful in small spaces. This model, of standard worktop height, has a deep drawer, a hanging rail for utensils, and a pull-out shelf.

## WORKTOP HEIGHT

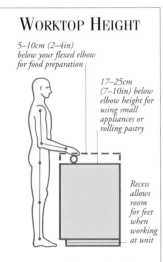

*5–10cm (2–4in) below your flexed elbow for food preparation*

*17–25cm (7–10in) below elbow height for using small appliances or rolling pastry*

*Recess allows room for feet when working at unit*

Although kitchen worktops are a standard height, it is useful to have a lower surface for certain food preparation processes.

## REMEMBER

■ Make a realistic assessment of your cooking requirements and plan accordingly. If you live alone or cook very little, you may not need a traditional-format kitchen.

■ If you do not have room for even a table-top fridge, consider the possibility of storing fruit and vegetables in a larder or outside store where they will keep fresh for longer.

■ Combination ovens provide the speed and compact design of a microwave oven along with the advantages of a convection oven and grill.

■ Make sure that there is a heat-resistant surface next to the cooker so that hot pans will not cause damage.

■ Consider your shopping and cooking habits when buying a fridge or freezer, and choose a model that suits your lifestyle.

## TABLE-TOP APPLIANCES

An increasing choice of scaled-down, table-top versions of standard kitchen appliances, including fridges and cookers, is becoming available. To this can be added a range of table-cookers: electric grills and griddles, slow-cook woks, and even a mini electric oven that bakes, roasts, and grills.

△ CLASSIC COMPACT COOKER
Designed to sit on a kitchen worktop, or on an optional fold-flat stand, this updated version of a classic compact cooker includes two hot plates, an oven, and a grill.

△ TABLE-TOP SLOW COOKER
Slow cookers present great possibilities for imaginative and economical one-pan cooking, and many are attractive enough to be brought to the table for serving.

△ MINI FRIDGE
If space is tight, look for a mini fridge like this model, which features an ice-box, temperature control, and room for several bottles in the door, but is small enough to fit on a worktop.

# KITCHEN STORAGE SYSTEMS

When space is limited, it is vital that none of it is wasted or overlooked. The simple units designed originally for warehouse and factory use are especially space-saving, and have been successfully assimilated into domestic interiors. Make full use of wall and ceiling space: a ceiling rail with hooks provides convenient storage for saucepans and other cooking utensils.

WALL HANGING SYSTEMS ▷
Clear clutter off the worksurface and create more working space by hanging utensils on the walls. A wall-mounted rail and hook system offers flexibility by allowing pots and pans and cooking implements to be stored in the most convenient location.

*SAUCEPAN STAND*
*Make the most of a corner space with this multi-tiered saucepan stand.*

*HANGING UTENSILS*
*Essential cooking utensils hang on the wall above the hob.*

◁ VERTICAL SPACE
Vertical systems can provide a useful amount of kitchen storage while occupying minimal floor space. Consider narrow shelves or suspended tiers of wire vegetable baskets.

*DRAWER STORAGE*
*Infrequently used kitchen equipment is stored in drawer units next to and underneath the built-in oven.*

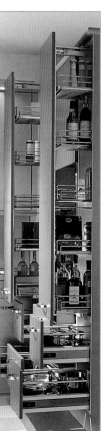

△ AWKWARD CORNER
A corner space becomes easily accessible with pull-out cantilevered trays. Use the space to store bulky saucepans and infrequently used kitchen equipment.

PULL-OUT LARDER ▷
Pull-out storage units with adjustable shelves maximize deep wall space. Designed to carry heavy loads, they hold a surprising number of packets and cans.

FLEXIBLE WALL SYSTEM ▷
Modular wall storage systems provide the opportunity to select and arrange components according to individual taste and requirements, as well as being a convenient, easily accessible method of storage.

Functional items, such as spice jars, oil and vinegar bottles, cutlery baskets, pots of growing herbs, kitchen-roll holders, and bunches of garlic can all be displayed, along with purely decorative items.

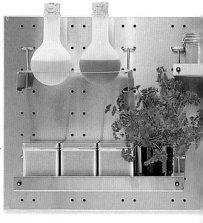

# WASHING-UP AND WASTE DISPOSAL

Manufacturers have responded to the needs of people living on their own in small spaces by producing worktop mini dishwashers and ultra-slim models that fit underneath counters, as well as ingenious space-saving sinks. Waste disposal units are ideal for high-rise dwellers, but they require correctly sized waste pipes and a second sink to work effectively.

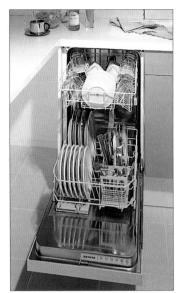

◁ **DISHWASHER**
Dealing immediately with dirty dishes and pans helps to keep a small living space tidy. Dishwashers designed to sit on a kitchen worktop, yet offering a normal range of washing and drying options, provide one solution to the problem.

△ **SLIMLINE DISHWASHER**
This compact dishwasher is ideal for studio living and can be slotted into a narrow gap beneath a kitchen worktop, provided the water supply and water pipes are within reach.

**ADAPTABLE KITCHEN SINK** ▽
Look for sinks that offer a choice of accessories such as extra worksurfaces and draining baskets. To satisfy the growing consumer demand for colours, traditional stainless steel sinks are now being challenged by sculptural designs in composite resin that feels like ceramic.

*DISH RACK*
*An efficient metal drainer fits over the sink instead of taking up worktop space.*

*VERSATILE DRAINER*
*This two-sectioned plastic drainer is a practical and space-saving device.*

*SPICE SHELF*
*Jars of colourful spices provide an attractive and useful display.*

*WALL PANEL*
*Specially designed for small spaces, this system consists of a stainless steel wall panel and a range of hooks, bars, and shelves.*

◁ **WASTE DISPOSAL**
An alternative to the free-standing waste bin or door-hung, swing-out bin, this unusual yet simple method for disposing of organic waste can be adapted to fit under existing worktops.

**RECYCLING WASTE** ▷
With the growing trend for separating and recycling kitchen waste – and for keen gardeners who choose to make their own compost – separate bins to hold organic and inorganic matter are indispensable.

# DINING AREA

THE EXTENT OF YOUR ENJOYMENT of food and cooking, and your preference for eating at speed or dining at leisure, must exert a strong influence on your choice of furniture and fittings for this area. But, with planning and imagination, the difficulties of eating and entertaining in a tight space can be resolved, so that dirty dishes are quickly cleared from view and extra tables and chairs can be folded away or stacked in a corner when not in use.

## VERSATILE BREAKFAST BARS

If you prefer a simple, informal eating area for everyday use, breakfast bars provide a neat and space-efficient option. Choose from a traditional, fixed peninsular bar, a kitchen counter with diner-style high stools – which may partially separate the cooking and living areas – or a hinged, wall-hung table that can be fitted in any suitable wall space and supported by a leg or a bracket that folds flat after use. If possible, site your breakfast bar where you can enjoy the morning sun.

△ PULL-OUT BREAKFAST BAR
Concealed behind a false drawer front, this pull-out breakfast bar with drop-down leg supports is an ingenious extension of the worktop. It can be quickly set up, and concealed when not in use, yet takes up only the space of one drawer in a standard kitchen unit.

◁ **CORNER TABLE FOR TWO**
When living in a restricted space, do not overlook any space, however small or awkwardly shaped: small tables can be designed to fit into the most surprising places. This example, supported on one leg, is built into a small, unused corner space.

▽ **HIGH-TECH SOLUTION**
An elegant method of concealing the cooking area in a studio or loft is to install a blind. In this high-tech loft, the kitchen area is screened off by a remote-controlled aluminium venetian blind. A dramatic lighting effect is created by switching on the kitchen counter downlighters when the blind is lowered.

## FOLDING AND STACKING TABLES AND CHAIRS

Furniture that can be packed away saves a lot of space and reduces clutter, while a block of colourful stacking chairs can form an attractive interior feature. Folding chairs can be propped against the wall or hung decoratively on hooks or Shaker peg rails, liberating valuable floor space. Echoes of camping equipment are evident in these designs, which are based on adaptability and the use of strong, lightweight materials.

*STACKING CHAIRS*
*Several of these chairs can be stored in a small area.*

**SUPPLEMENTARY SEATING** △
Stacking chairs are a neat solution to additional seating requirements for those living in small spaces.

*EASY STORAGE*
*A folding table can be propped against the wall or stored in a cupboard when not in use, while stacking chairs take up little space.*

◁ **LIGHTWEIGHT FURNITURE**
A lightweight aluminium folding table and stacking chairs, which complement the aluminium blinds running the length of this minimalist loft, can be easily hidden away after use, leaving the uncluttered spaciousness of the apartment to be appreciated.

### REMEMBER

■ Choose a kitchen bar for convenient everyday eating, bringing out a folding or trestle table for more formal dining.

■ Try to position the dining area in the sunniest part of the room to benefit from the morning or afternoon light.

■ Analyse your cooking and eating patterns carefully, and select furniture accordingly.

■ Look for imaginative ways of screening off the cooking area and of storing tables and chairs when they are not in use.

**OUTDOOR-INDOOR EATING** ▷
Garden-style folding furniture, bathed in light streaming through the full-width window, creates a sense of the outdoor patio area extending into the interior.

# WORK AREA

THE KEY TO WORKING FROM HOME, when space is limited or shared, is an efficient filing system that allows the work area to be kept as tidy and contained as possible. A home office can be built from a combination of fixed and mobile units, or you may choose a hinged, fold-away desk, a simple worktop on trestles, or even a traditional bureau with a drop-down surface.

## FLEXIBLE WORKSTATIONS

A work unit that can be easily moved out of sight or folded away when not in use makes an ideal home office in a restricted living space. Look for a design that will provide ample storage space for all your work-related equipment, files, and accessories, as well as features such as pull-out sections and adjustable shelving for maximum flexibility.

**HOME OFFICE ▷**
Constructed from MDF (medium-density fibreboard) and translucent plastic on a steel frame, this ingenious home office provides storage for computer equipment and files in the door section, and a pivoting, adjustable shelf to hold a computer monitor. The whole unit can be closed up when not in use.

**HINGED DESK ▷**
Two hinged surfaces – one providing the work area, the other providing its support – fold flat against the wall when not in use. This imaginative idea, although simple and inexpensive, provides a generous amount of work space when required, yet takes up very little room when folded away.

**MONITOR POSITION**
*To prevent eye-strain, adjust the position of your screen to suit your height and line of vision.*

**PIVOTING BASE**
*An adjustable base allows the position of the monitor to be easily changed.*

**SWIVEL SUPPORT**
*Further flexibility in positioning the monitor is provided by the swivelling steel support.*

**COMPUTER STORAGE**
*A computer is stored vertically in one of the internal door sections.*

**OUT OF SIGHT**
*The unit, on castors for easy mobility, closes to form a neat "cube".*

**PULL-OUT PRINTER SHELF**
*The sliding shelf, holding a printer or other peripheral device, can be pushed back when not in use.*

◁ **CONCEALED DESK**
When the hinged work surface and its support are folded away, the desk is concealed, leaving an uncluttered space in front of the kitchen work area.

*FOLD-AWAY SURFACE*
*The work surface folds flat against the back of the kitchen unit.*

*FOLD-AWAY SUPPORT*
*The desk is supported by a hinged panel.*

*VERTICAL SPACE*
*Two narrow shelves, one above the other, provide storage space for a surprising number of vertical files.*

*WORKSTATION*
*Variously sized shelves hold all the equipment required in home computing.*

## SPACE-SAVING COMPUTER TROLLEY △
Computer trolleys, designed to hold computer, monitor, keyboard, printer, and other equipment, are widely available and, like this lightweight, painted steel model, have the advantage of being easily moved out of sight when not in use. They can also be used to hold a television set or sound system.

# FILING SYSTEMS

A wide choice of filing and work storage systems is available, including wall-hung, stacking, and mobile units. Vertically arranged designs offer the maximum storage capacity while occupying the least amount of floor space; multi-functional mobile units are also useful in tight spaces.

*WALL UNIT*
*Make good use of odd spaces with a narrow wall unit.*

*AT A GLANCE*
*Visible and accessible work tools make for smooth-running, stress-free work.*

*EASY MOBILITY*
*Storage on wheels can be easily pushed away or turned around.*

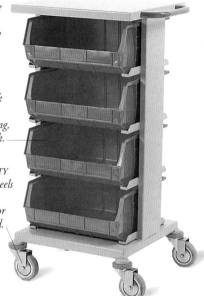

△ **VERTICAL POCKETS**
Made of galvanized metal, this slim, vertical pocket system will fit into the narrowest gap, yet provides useful space for storage or display. A horizontal version is just as effective.

△ **MOBILE STORAGE SYSTEM**
Industrial storage systems often include well-designed, robustly constructed units that are ideal for the home office. This useful storage trolley, with open-fronted, pull-out drawers can be easily moved around.

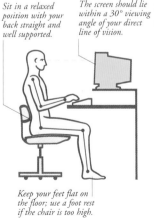

*SPLASH OF COLOUR*
*Painted and lacquered MDF (medium-density fibreboard), provides the colour in this functional design.*

*STEADY WORK*
*Castors with brakes prevent the unit from moving while work is in progress.*

## WORKING POSITION

*Sit in a relaxed position with your back straight and well supported.*

*The screen should lie within a 30° viewing angle of your direct line of vision.*

*Keep your feet flat on the floor; use a foot rest if the chair is too high.*

When work involves sitting at a desk for long periods, good posture and correct positioning of equipment are vital.

**FIBREBOARD BOXES △**
These durable black fibreboard boxes are available in a variety of sizes and designs, and form part of a range of containers that can be used individually or stacked.

## REMEMBER

■ Look for flexible, space-saving systems, such as stacking boxes of all sizes, wall-mounted plastic tray systems, and stacking units on wheels.

■ Give a new lease of life to a secondhand metal filing cabinet by respraying it in a colour to match your decor.

■ Don't put design and style before personal comfort. Make sure that monitor, desk, chair, and keyboard heights are all correctly adjusted.

■ Enhance your living space by hiding unattractive office equipment behind cupboard doors or screens.

# WASHING AREA

WHEN PLANNING YOUR BATHROOM, think beyond the limitations of the existing hot and cold water supply and waste stack positions: pipework can always be moved, thereby providing many new possibilities for the location and size of your washing area. Choose from a wide variety of space-efficient designs – from corner baths and showers to modern sitz baths.

## BATHS AND SHOWERS

Showers are convenient, economical, fast, and ideal in restricted spaces. For those who prefer a relaxing bath, however, a range of ingenious designs allows a tub to be fitted into the most awkward area. Some baths are wider at one end than the other, while others fit neatly across a corner.

**SHOWER-ROOM ▷**
Although there is enough space to fit a bath in this high-tech shower-room, with its salvaged steel basin and exposed pipework, the entire width has been fitted instead with a custom-made steel shower tray, with an extra-large shower rose. A frosted glass panel allows natural light to enter.

**CREATIVE SOLUTION ▷**
This sunken bath is a unique space-saving feature: with the bed rolled back and the blinds down, a private bathing area is created, with interesting light effects produced by the underwater lighting. There is generous storage space beneath the decking constructed from reclaimed Scottish pitch pine.

### REMEMBER

■ When choosing a shower, check that the unit suits the water pressure and flow rate of your plumbing system.

■ Discuss your bathroom plans with a qualified plumber and electrician before starting work.

■ Standards for WC valves vary from country to country, so check that you have selected an appropriate system.

■ Remember to leave adequate space for movement around each piece of equipment.

■ A ventilation fan must be fitted in an internal bathroom or shower-room to prevent damp and condensation.

■ Hide the unsightly clutter of pipework and cisterns behind fitted cupboards and semi-recessed vanity units.

■ Enjoy the free luxury of washing in sunlight by clever positioning of a shower or bath.

■ When planning a bathroom, consider the benefit of fitting a heated towel rail.

**CORNER SHOWER UNIT △**
Showers are ideal when space is limited, as they can be fitted into any corner or incorporated into wardrobe units. Shower panels must be made of toughened safety glass.

## CLEVER BASINS

Basins come in an exciting variety of shapes and sizes, as well as being made of different materials, but in small bathrooms it is crucial that you select a model that is large enough for your needs yet avoids wasting space. For example, a basin can be wall-hung on brackets or semi-recessed into a cupboard unit, both options allowing for storage space below.

**SWIVEL BASIN**
*When the WC is in use, the basin is swivelled to one side.*

**SHARED SPACE**
*The handbasin fits neatly above the WC.*

**ADAPTABLE DESIGN** △
The pre-plumbed panel of this clever, space-saving unit with swivelling handbasin contains hot and cold water and waste pipes, and allows for an individual choice of basin and WC to be installed.

**REMOVABLE LEGS**
*The legs can be removed and the bath fitted into a built-in unit.*

**SPACE-SAVING BATH** △
Providing a compromise between a shower and a bath when space is limited, the sitz bath is an option for those who prefer bathing in comfort. Traditional in design, it takes up little space and is ideal for a small bathroom, bedroom, or even under the stairs.

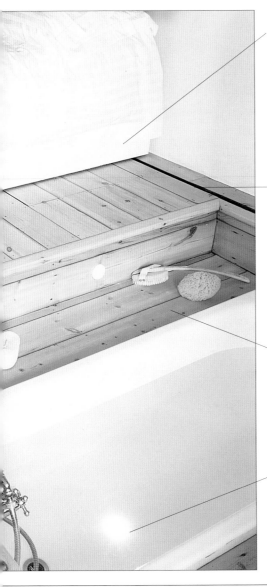

**UNDER-BED STORAGE**
*Deep storage drawers are built into the space beneath the double bed.*

**SMOOTH MOVEMENT**
*The rubber rollers of the bed run in channels, making it easy to move despite its weight.*

**BATH SHELF**
*A generous shelf space for storing toiletries has been built around the bath, like the deck of a boat.*

**BATH LIGHT**
*The bath water, lit up by an underwater light installed in the base, throws reflections onto the ceiling.*

**BRIGHT CORNER**
*White paint and a sunny position ensure that this corner is bright with reflected light.*

**EXTRA STORAGE**
*Additional storage space has been created under the vanity basin in the remodelled wall.*

△ **CREATIVE WALLS**
This wall looks like an original feature, but it has been newly constructed, with a small vanity basin, glass shelf, and cupboard built into an alcove where they are almost invisible from the rest of the studio apartment.

# SLEEPING AREA

MANY OF THE IDEAS for fitting beds into small spaces, such as the truckle bed or the Japanese futon, are based on traditional designs. Other space-saving solutions, such as fold-away beds and raised beds with lockers below, originate from cabin and couchette fittings. A major question is whether the bed has to double as another piece of furniture, such as seating, during the day, or whether it can be be concealed when not in use.

*SIMPLE STORAGE*
*On the reverse side to the bed is a storage unit for TV and audio equipment.*

## FOLD-DOWN BEDS

The main advantage of a bed that folds up into the wall during the daytime is that it frees a considerable amount of living space. The bed is concealed behind a vertical surface that can then be used for decorative purposes. The disadvantage is that bedding must be packed away when the bed is not in use, which may prove inconvenient when carried out on a daily basis.

*ADAPTABLE SCREEN/BED ▷*
A good example of an adaptable, multi-purpose design, this screen/bed has shelving for audio equipment, CDs, and magazines on one side and, on the other, a hydraulically operated, pull-down bed. Pivoting side units on either side of the bed open out to create a contained sleeping area behind the screen, which is finished on both sides with a decorative panelled effect.

*HANGING SPACE*
*Hooks set into the angled roof space create a small front-facing wardrobe.*

*DOOR SHELVING*
*The interior surface of the wardrobe door is fitted with useful storage shelves.*

*PAINTED MDF*
*The main structure of the unit is made from medium-density fibreboard (MDF).*

*EASY OPENING*
*A hydraulic system enables the bed panel to be opened and closed with ease.*

### CONCEALED BED AND WARDROBE △
The pull-down bed and the wardrobe next to it are both completely concealed behind large panels. These have been treated with a special Italian-style tinted plaster finish to provide a neutral backdrop for furniture. The bed alcove, which includes a shelf for books and alarm clock, is illuminated by halogen spotlights.

*PIVOTING UNITS*
*The side units pivot outwards, supported on rubber-tyred castors, to provide useful bedside storage.*

**BED CLOSED**
*The bed is folded up
and the side units closed.*

**PANELLED EFFECT**
*A decorative effect is
achieved by covering
the vertical panels
with squares of 5mm
(³/₁₆in) MDF.*

**TRANSLUCENT BACK**
*The side units and a
small bedhead alcove
are backed with
translucent plastic.*

# DUAL-PURPOSE BEDS

A bed is one of the most important and one of the largest items in any living space so, when space is limited, it is vital to choose one that earns its keep by doubling as seating or storage – or both – during the day, as well as providing a comfortable place to sleep at night.

**VENTILATED BASE**
*Air circulates
through holes to
the foam mattress
stored within.*

**BED SUPPORT**
*The hardwood
end pieces double
as frame supports
when the bed is
unfolded.*

△ **MULTI-FUNCTIONAL BENCH-BED**
Based on the delightfully simple principle of a box with a hinged lid, this space-saving bed, constructed in painted MDF with hardwood legs, can be used as a bench, a display shelf, or as a low table.

△ **ROOM WITHIN A ROOM**
The construction of this softwood platform bed has created generous study space below, with room for shelving and storage units.

▽ **UNDERBED STORAGE**
The space beneath a bed is ideal for storage – whether in deep drawers, mobile containers, or zipped bags – or, as here, for a spare bed.

**HINGED BASE BOARD**
*When the bed is folded up
this base board hangs flat.*

**TRUCKLE BED**
*Underneath this elegant, veneered and
painted daybed is a pull-out truckle bed on
collapsible legs, disguised as a drawer.*

# UTILITY AREA

CLEVER MECHANISMS AND FITTINGS provide the key to storing basic appliances and cleaning equipment so that they are easily accessible, but do not create unsightly clutter in a restricted living space. Indeed, the quality of life in one-room living depends very much on such hidden services. Concealed or not, however, stored objects are usable only if they are tidily organized in a practical, modular storage system.

## STORING EQUIPMENT

Solutions to storing cleaning equipment range from simple, imaginative ideas to integrated appliances. Industrial systems such as pull-out larder units, which were formerly found only in warehouses and factories, are now being appropriated by the domestic market because they are so practical and use a minimum of materials.

### WIRE RACK STORAGE SYSTEMS ▷

In restricted areas, wire rack and basket systems provide an invaluable and flexible method of storage. They can be fitted into virtually any space, whether under the stairs or on the backs of cupboard doors. They do not gather dust and everything that is stored is immediately visible and accessible. Hooks and small containers can be added to extend their storage possibilities.

---

### REMEMBER

■ Reduce clutter by fitting racks and baskets, hooks, and hanging pockets on the backs of cupboard doors and inside any useful concealed space

■ Make the best use of hard-to-reach corner spaces under worktops by installing carousel storage trays.

■ Store dusters and shoe-cleaning equipment in bags hung inside cupboards.

■ Good ventilation is vital for cupboards where cleaning equipment is stored.

■ Marine-grade plywood, being impervious to moisture and steam, is an ideal material to use in badly ventilated small kitchens and washing areas.

---

*NO CLUTTER*
*Use wall brackets and clips to hold vacuum cleaners, extension tubes, and tools neatly in place.*

*SPACE SAVERS*
*Wire racks, of stainless steel or plastic-coated wire, are widely available in a range of designs.*

*LARGE ITEMS*
*Ensure that there is room for large items such as a vacuum cleaner ironing board, and buckets.*

◁ SIMPLE SOLUTIONS
One cheap and cheerful solution to storage is a simple fabric "shoebag" that can be hung up wherever there is space. Other inexpensive ideas include colourful plastic baskets and stacking boxes and crates.

▽ **BELOW-STAIRS UTILITY ROOM**
Despite its location under the stairs, this utility room –
which houses a washer-dryer as well as other essential
household equipment – appears spacious. The bright
colour scheme and the full-width mirror in the adjacent
washing area not only help to create an airy feeling, but
also seem to double the size of this internal room.

# LAUNDRY FACILITIES

The requirements of people living alone or in
small spaces has resulted in a new generation
of compact washing and drying machines.
When teamed with retractable ironing boards
and high-level clothes-drying rails, these basic
services take up very little space and may even
be concealed entirely from view.

◁ **MINI WASHER**
Compact clothes-
washing machines,
which are designed to
sit on a sink drainer
and to be put away
when not in use, are
ideal for those living
in restricted spaces.

*SINK-TOP WASHING*
*Easily connected to a*
*hot water supply, this*
*top-loading machine*
*is simple to use.*

△ **SLIMLINE MODEL**
Ideal for fitting into a small
utility cupboard or narrow
space, a slimline washing
machine takes up much less
room than a standard front-
loading model.

**TRADITIONAL PULLEY** △
A simple rise-and-fall "pulley",
made of plastic-coated steel or
natural wood, provides one of
the most space-saving methods
of drying and airing laundry.

**HANGING BRACKETS** ▷
When space is restricted, hang
appliances on the wall rather
than prop them up. Look for
suitable brackets in industrial
catalogues or ironmongers.

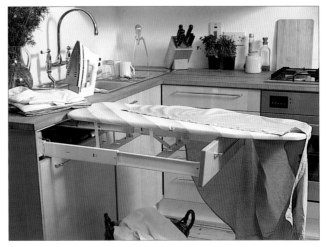

△ **FOLD-AWAY IRONING BOARD**
Stored behind a false drawer front in a sink unit, this pull-out,
folding ironing board includes an extra extension for ironing sleeves.
The telescopic supporting brackets are part of an extensive range of
mechanisms designed to allow fold-away appliances to be integrated
into your own choice of cupboard or drawer units.

# SPACE DIVIDERS

AREAS OF PRIVACY can be achieved in a single living space by a clever use of screening devices. Draped translucent fabric, blinds, sliding or opening panels, and simple folding screens are the traditional methods. Mobile storage units offer a flexible approach to dividing spaces, while remote-controlled, aluminium venetian blinds add a dramatic high-tech touch.

## MULTI-PURPOSE ROOM DIVIDERS

Screens and panels make excellent room dividers but, when using them in a limited space, be sure to make the most of both sides: the front and back can be treated in different ways, either decoratively or as a support for shelving, cupboards, or clothes hanging rails.

**△ SLIDING DOORS**
Sliding doors and panels take up less space than double or folding doors. These top-hung panels, which are fitted from top to bottom with shelves to maximize their use, glide together to block off the work space on the far side.

**"SCREENROBE" ▷**
Today's designers are producing inventive solutions to the problems of small-space living, such as this dual-purpose, cherry-wood wardrobe with maple-veneered MDF (medium-density fibreboard) doors and hinged side screens. In this version, two units – one with shelves and the other with hanging space – stand together; the folding panels at either side can be opened to create a simple screen, or closed and folded flat against the wardrobe.

*WARDROBE*
*With the screens closed, the unit is a wardrobe with plentiful shelving and storage space.*

*SCREEN*
*With the side panels open, and wardrobe doors closed, a solid screen is formed.*

*HANGING RAIL*
*A movable rail can be pulled to the outside of the wardrobe behind the screen, providing useful hanging space and a dressing area.*

*HINGED PANELS*
*The side panels are hinged to open outwards, and to fold flat against the sides of the wardrobe.*

*EASY MOVING*
*A vertically sliding leg allows the screen panel to be positioned on an uneven surface.*

# SCREENS AND BLINDS

There are many ways of creating screens: Japanese-style sliding screens and natural bamboo blinds can form space-saving room dividers, while reflective aluminium slatted blinds offer a stylish alternative. Translucent materials, including fabrics such as muslin or silk, plastics, glass bricks, and sand-blasted glass, are ideal for allowing light into internal spaces without loss of privacy.

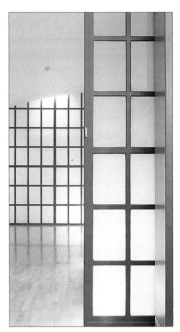

◁ **HIGH-TECH SCREEN**
This remote-controlled aluminium venetian blind is one of several used to divide the space in a loft apartment. The screen is light and reflective, so the interior space created does not appear boxed in.

**TRANSLUCENT SCREENING** ▽
It is important, in one-room living, to maintain a sense of space and light, and this is achieved here by using a translucent screen to separate what might otherwise remain a dark understairs area.

△ **MAXIMIZING LIGHT**
Sand-blasted glass is an attractive option for fixed and sliding screens. It makes the most of the available natural light by subtle transmission and diffusion and also permits the creation of ever-changing patterns of light and shadow, which help to enliven flat surfaces.

# STORAGE

ORDER IN THE HOME relies on an efficient, well-organized storage system. Modular units, which can be acquired gradually and arranged according to individual taste and changing needs, are particularly useful, while hanging storage can be used to fill awkward spaces. Storage ranged along an entire wall can, surprisingly, create rather than reduce space.

## WALL-MOUNTED UNITS

In small apartments it is essential to fit storage on the walls as far as possible in order to free floor space for general living. Wall systems range from pockets and adjustable shelves to peg-boards, brackets, and butcher's hooks, and they can be fitted onto any available wall space using the appropriate fixings.

◁ WALL-HUNG LETTER/MAGAZINE RACK
Vertical storage racks are practical and space-saving and can be fixed at any height, in any area of the room. This letter rack was designed for office use but it is equally suited to the storage of magazines and correspondence at home.

*VERTICAL STORAGE*
*Made in natural plywood with steel rods, this rack is suitable for any narrow wall space.*

*ADJUSTABLE SHELVES*
*The shelves on this unit can be moved up and down the pillar. They are suitable for any narrow space.*

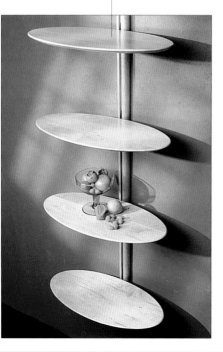

WALL-HUNG
SHELVING UNIT ▷
For maximum flexibility look for adjustable, wall-hung shelving units such as these practical and decorative maplewood shelves, which can be easily moved up and down the single, wall-mounted pillar.

## STACKING SYSTEMS

When space is limited, modular stacking units provide a neat solution to storage problems. Whether you opt for the simple method of piling matching boxes, baskets, tins, or crates on top of each other, or invest in a customized unit to suit the space available and your particular storage requirements, stacking systems provide one of the most efficient ways of fitting the maximum amount of storage into even the most restricted space.

*INEXPENSIVE CRATES*
*These plastic crates provide a practical way to store items that need ventilation, such as towels and linen.*

PLASTIC CONTAINERS ▷
Plastic storage units range from inexpensive stacking crates to mobile trolley units with plastic trays that can be added on as required. These offer a flexible method of storing anything from clothing to household supplies.

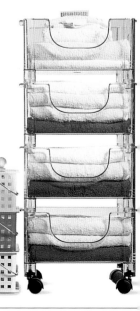

# FLEXIBLE FABRIC STORAGE

Hanging wardrobes are just one of the wide and ingenious range of storage containers made from cotton or canvas. Many of these products are ideal for small-space living: they are inexpensive, adaptable in their use, and they can be fitted into odd corners. Fabric wall pockets and hanging "shelves" are particularly useful for storing small items in an organized way.

△ CANVAS SELF-ASSEMBLY WARDROBES
Easily assembled, both of these wardrobes are made of canvas. One, on a steel frame, is zip-fronted; the other has a plastic frame and roll-up front, with a floor-level shelf for shoes.

CANVAS SHELVES △
Simple and versatile, these space-saving, hanging canvas shelves for shoes, jumpers, and underwear are simply attached to the rail with a sturdy Velcro fastening.

△ BASKET STORAGE
Wicker baskets are available in various sizes and provide a light, inexpensive, and portable method of storage that suits interiors with a natural, homely feel.

▽ SPACE-SAVING SYSTEM
Components of this type of metal system can be bought separately and assembled to suit your needs. The whole arrangement can be open or fitted into a cupboard.

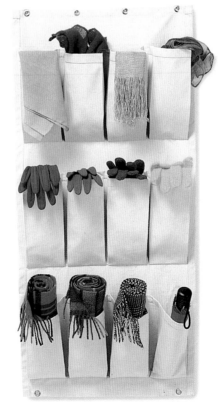

HANGING POCKETS △
A set of twelve cotton pockets, attached to a door, wall, or cupboard, can be used to store anything from scarves and gloves to cleaning equipment or shoes.

## REMEMBER

■ Stackability is the guiding principle when looking for storage containers.

■ Choose storage units in a style and finish appropriate to the space. Natural materials like bamboo and cotton possess a timeless quality, while plastics add a splash of intense colour.

■ Salvage sturdy, secondhand cabinets from offices and shops. Spray with a coat of paint and attach new handles.

■ Look for flexible, modular systems that allow units to be fitted into awkward spaces.

# BUILT-IN STORAGE

To be successful, built-in storage should merge unobtrusively into the structure of the interior. The first task is to locate all unused spaces. If your room has high ceilings, consider constructing a false, suspended ceiling that will provide a large "attic" space; in the same way, useful underfloor storage can be created by raising the floor level. False walls, lined with shelving and cupboards, can hold a vast amount of storage, especially if teamed with pull-out fittings.

*CELLAR SPACE*
*Opening this hatch reveals that the below-floor space has become a "cellar" holding a large amount of long-term storage.*

**UNDERFLOOR SPACE ▷**
The construction of a raised platform or false floor can create, at the same time, new areas of storage space. In this example, storage has even been incorporated into the step leading from one floor level to another.

*TOOL CHEST*
*The space below this step, leading from one floor level to the next, is not wasted, but forms an easily accessible tool chest.*

△ **BUILT-IN DRESSING ROOM**
As well as a useful laundry chute and a vanity cupboard, this brightly painted built-in wardrobe, adjacent to a raised sleeping area, contains a vertical shoe store and a pull-out clothes hanging rail.

## REMEMBER

■ As far as possible, use "dead" and wasted space, especially narrow "in-between" spaces, corners, underfloor areas, and even underneath stair treads.

■ Unused wall space above WCs, along corridors, in entrance lobbies, and above windows can all be usefully fitted with storage.

■ Pack items for long-term storage in dustproof containers and ensure that environmental conditions are suitable.

■ Attic space is particularly valuable for storing possessions on a long-term basis.

**WALL-TO-WALL STORAGE ▷**
One of the best uses of space is to line an entire wall with a built-in storage unit. Not only can it hold all your possessions and keep the floor clear, but it also makes the interior appear larger.

△ **INTEGRAL SHELF STORAGE**
A vast quantity of books and boxes is stored in these shelves, which have been built in alongside the steps leading to a raised area in a loft apartment. Painted bright yellow, they appear as one neat storage unit.

# LONG-TERM STORAGE

Make use of high-level spaces for the long-term storage of infrequently used items, such as seasonal clothes and do-it-yourself equipment, and consider whether you need to provide permanently fixed access or a ladder that can be put away when not in use. If you are planning to remodel a room, this is an ideal opportunity to anticipate your needs and build in as much storage space as possible.

*HANDY STOOL*
*When folded away, these steps double as a useful stool.*

*EASY STEPS*
*The two steps pivot smoothly out from under the stool.*

△ **FOLD-AWAY STEPS**
Dual-purpose steps such as these, which double as a stool or side table, are useful in a small studio. Library steps that turn into a chair are a more traditional version.

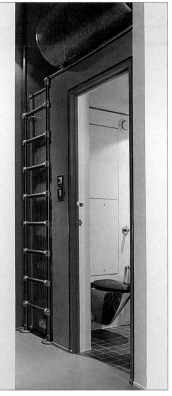

△ **VERTICAL RUNGS**
This ladder, with each rung attached individually to the wall, leads to a high-level area above the bathroom. A sheet of transparent acrylic protects the painted wall from scuff marks.

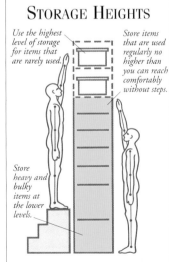

## STORAGE HEIGHTS

*Use the highest level of storage for items that are rarely used.*

*Store items that are used regularly no higher than you can reach comfortably without steps.*

*Store heavy and bulky items at the lower levels.*

Store heavy objects at low level, and label boxes on high-level shelves with listed contents to avoid unnecessary searching.

△ **HIGH-LEVEL STORAGE**
Loft space in an adjacent corridor is reached through a trap-door in the living area of this apartment, with a ladder providing the means of access.

# FLOORING

THE CHOICE OF FLOORING can completely transform a room, but your decision must encompass practical considerations, such as cost and the extent of use in different areas, as well as personal style preferences. Lofts tend to feature hard finishes – exposed brick, concrete, and timber floors – which increase sound levels, but these can be muted by adding rugs and other resilient materials. Underfloor heating, which is enjoying a revival, is compatible with most types of floor coverings, but is particularly efficient with ceramic, stone, and well-seasoned hardwood.

## TEXTURED RUBBER

Available as sheet or tiles, natural or synthetic (or a blend of the two), rubber is both hard-wearing and decorative.

### ADVANTAGES
• Durable and easy to clean.
• Quiet, resilient, and non-slip.
• Exciting range of colours, effects, and patterns.

### DISADVANTAGES
• Shows scratches, but they can fade with time.
• Dark scuff marks can be obvious.

**FLOORING AS A ROOM DIVIDER**
A change of colour and texture is an effective way of defining two different areas in a single space.

## COLOUR-WASHED WOOD

Wood has its own charm, but a soft paint wash can brighten up weathered boards or mask poor-quality timber.

### ADVANTAGES
• You control the colour depth and tone.
• Colour can be re-applied at any time.
• Compatible with underfloor heating.

### DISADVANTAGES
• Expands in reaction to water and humidity.
• Is not impact-resistant and can splinter.
• Tends to amplify sound levels.

## ASSESS YOUR FLOORING NEEDS

■ Do you want to visually separate each living area or would you prefer the whole interior to form one spatial flow? Use flooring finishes to achieve different effects.

■ Are you planning neutral-coloured walls to create a feeling of space? A natural-coloured floor will help to add warmth.

■ Would you like to create space by dispensing with visible radiators? Underfloor heating provides an alternative, but check that flooring is suitable.

■ Does the luxury of walking on carpet appeal to you? If so, have you considered how much cleaning and maintenance it requires, and whether it is practical in all areas?

■ Do you like the clean lines of wooden flooring? Remember that real wood can be replaced by remarkably convincing vinyl or laminate.

■ If you like plain-coloured flooring, have you considered that it shows up marks more quickly than a patterned surface?

# TEXTURED VINYL

Sheet vinyl (PVC) is tough, waterproof, and non-slip, and is available in a wide range of colours and textures.

### ADVANTAGES
• Feels warm and absorbs sound.
• Durable and requires minimal maintenance.
• Easy to cut round awkwardly shaped walls.

### DISADVANTAGES
• May be marked by furniture without castors.
• Can be stained by shoe polish and fibre pens.

# NATURAL FIBRE MATTING

Plant-fibre matting, such as seagrass, coir, sisal, or jute, offers a warm, natural look and can be loose laid or fitted.

### ADVANTAGES
• Hard-wearing and sound-absorbent.
• Decorative weaves and colours available.
• A natural alternative to carpet and synthetics.

### DISADVANTAGES
• Borders must be bound to prevent fraying.
• Not suitable for kitchens or in direct sunlight.

# WOOD LAMINATE

Made from pressed, resin-impregnated papers, laminates offer an immense variety of colours, patterns, and textures.

### ADVANTAGES
• Extremely hard-wearing and durable.
• Hygienic, stain-resistant, and easy to maintain.
• Patterns and colours do not fade.

### DISADVANTAGES
• Hard surfaces can be noisy.
• More difficult to repair than carpet or vinyl.

# VINYL TILES

With all the advantages of sheet vinyl, vinyl tiles are available in a range of colours and can look good anywhere.

### ADVANTAGES
• Spare tiles can be kept to repair worn areas.
• You can create your own unique pattern.
• Tiles are quick and easy to lay.

### DISADVANTAGES
• Corners may break if not stuck down firmly.
• May not be waterproof if edges are not close.
• Can be stained by waxes, polishes, and solvents.

# CARPET

Carpeting varies from expensive wool mixtures to cheaper synthetic blends, but all offer great comfort underfoot.

### ADVANTAGES
• Range of finishes from velvet to shag pile.
• Unlimited choice of colours and patterns.
• Damaged carpet can be easily replaced.

### DISADVANTAGES
• Regular cleaning needed to prolong carpet life.
• May need periodical re-stretching.
• Synthetic fibres react badly to burns.

# LINOLEUM

Made from almost 100% natural raw materials, linoleum is tough, durable, flexible, and easily maintained.

### ADVANTAGES
• Is a good insulator for airborne sound.
• Is comfortable to stand on, with a slight "give".
• Very hygienic and resistant to bacterial growth.

### DISADVANTAGES
• Can react to excessive water spills and seepage.
• Has a natural oily odour, which fades in time.
• Chairs must be fitted with soft castors.

# LIGHTING

LIGHTING CAN BE DRAMATIC OR SUBTLE. It can draw the eye towards a particular focus or make parts of a room disappear. Even a dimmer switch can completely alter an interior space. The ideal is a balance between ambient and task lighting, but lights should always be selected with a specific function in mind, and knowing their effect on surrounding surfaces and materials. The days of the single, central pendant bulb are long gone, and a stream of exciting, adaptable systems offer scope for imaginative ideas for shaping space and providing a good level of visibility.

## FLOOR-STANDING LAMP

The universal joint connecting the arm to the support of this simple, elegant lamp provides maximum flexibility.

**ADVANTAGES**
• Light can be directed to where it is needed.
• Height and angle of light are easily adjusted.
• Ideal as a floor-standing reading light.

**DISADVANTAGES**
• Light is not easily directed upwards.
• Trailing flex can be hazardous.

**COMBINATION OF LIGHTING**
A variety of lights, including uplighters, ceiling light, and wall-mounted spot, define different areas.

## ANGLEPOISE

Precisely balanced, either on a cast metal base or clamped to a work surface, this lamp is designed to rest in any position.

**ADVANTAGES**
• Ideal task light for working or reading.
• Can be angled to cast a pool of light.
• Very safe, weighty, cast metal base.

**DISADVANTAGES**
• Nuts holding light in position may loosen.
• The flex must be kept safely out of the way.
• Shade can become hot after lengthy use.

## ASSESS YOUR LIGHTING NEEDS

■ Make fixed lighting an important part of your scheme at the planning stage so that the electrical wiring system can be arranged before you start decorating. Sockets can then be added for lamps and lighting effects.

■ List special features or objects that you would like to be illuminated, such as a collection of glass or prints. Also make a note of wardrobes, kitchen cupboards, or storage spaces that need internal lighting. Make sure that food preparation areas are well lit.

■ Steps and entrances and access to raised platforms must be properly lit. Lights need not be wall- or ceiling-hung, but can be mounted at low levels so that the focus of illumination is on the stair-treads.

■ If your bed doubles as seating during the day, consider flexible lighting that will be suitable for both situations. Adjustable, Anglepoise-type lights, and clip-on, extending, and floor-standing lights are all adaptable and provide a good level of task lighting.

## PENDANT

The functional simplicity of this lamp fits in well with contemporary styling, and in particular with loft living.

ADVANTAGES
- Casts a cosy, friendly pool of light onto a table.
- Height can be adjusted to suit.
- Helps to create a focal point in the room.

DISADVANTAGES
- Requires a translucent bulb to avoid dazzle.
- Position of dining table is limited.

## CLIP-ON WORK LAMP

This very flexible lamp, which originated in a photographic studio, has now been adapted to suit any part of the home.

ADVANTAGES
- Can be clipped to any suitable fitting.
- Can provide ambient uplighting.
- Suitable as a bedside or worktop light.

DISADVANTAGES
- Trailing flex can be dangerous.
- Clip can mark wooden furniture.

## WALL-HUNG UPLIGHTER

Uplighters throw soft, reflected light around a room, creating ideal ambient lighting for living areas and relaxing.

ADVANTAGES
- Can enhance architectural features.
- Translucent shade produces diffused light.
- Bulb and wiring are concealed.

DISADVANTAGES
- Electrical wiring must be concealed.
- Not suitable for reading or working.

## MINI DOWNLIGHTERS

Low-voltage halogen fittings are now so small that they can be totally concealed in recesses on the underside of a shelf.

ADVANTAGES
- Are totally hidden and do not dazzle.
- Create bright, even lighting on worktops.
- Not hot enough to damage shelving.

DISADVANTAGES
- Difficult to conceal the wiring.
- A position has to be found for the transformer.
- Gloves needed to handle the bulbs.

## BARE-WIRE SYSTEM

Mini low-voltage halogen spotlights rest on parallel tensile wires, which act as the track between two points.

ADVANTAGES
- Lights can be easily moved along the cables.
- Halogen light has minimal effect on colours.
- Light can be directed onto a worktop.

DISADVANTAGES
- Transformer needed to convert electric current.
- Light can be dazzling.
- Transformer must be fitted by an electrician.

## EXTENDING LIGHT

Both practical and decorative, an extending light can provide a high level of light without causing eye-strain.

ADVANTAGES
- Light can be directed where needed.
- Lamp can be retracted when not in use.
- Can be angled to create a wash of light.

DISADVANTAGES
- Lamp will not stay in position if fittings loosen.
- Flex difficult to conceal.
- Clinical design may not suit all interiors.

ROOM PLANS

# LINEAR ROOM PLAN

THE 16-METRE-LONG INTERIOR SPACE in this late-nineteenth-century London interior allows the main functional areas to relate in one continuous and logical flow. The separate parts are defined by different floor finishes – sisal, antique Persian carpet, chequered vinyl, and natural wood – as well as by a progression of wall colours and finishes, including cool white and rich red paintwork, natural wood, and glass.

*Sleeping area*    *Living area*    *Boiler*    *Cooking area*    *Dining area*

— *Patio doors*

*Storage cupboard*

*Bathroom, with sleeping area above*

*Muslin screen*    *Entrance*    *Washing machine*

INTERNAL ROOM DIMENSIONS:
4m (12ft) WIDE
16m (48ft) LONG

**NO WASTED SPACE**
*Floor-to-ceiling shelving for books and other objects makes the best possible use of the available space.*

## △ BIRD'S EYE VIEW
The linear layout is a planner's dream: each of the functional areas is self-contained and distinct from its neighbour, yet forms part of the general flow.

## △ ❶ DRAMATIC DRAPERY
The dramatic view from the richly decorated living area towards the tranquil "bedroom" is framed by muslin drapes. These help to define and screen the sleeping area, as well as creating a calm and luminous effect in the morning light.

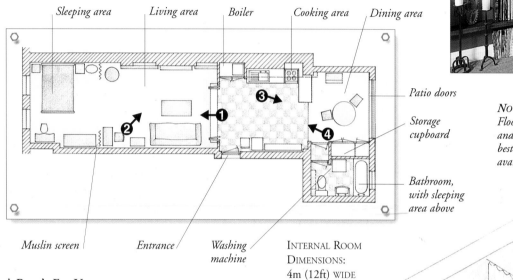

**STORAGE BASKETS**
*Wicker baskets provide versatile storage for bedlinen or laundry and complement the antique furnishings.*

**TRANSLUCENT SCREENING**
*Filmy white muslin provides an inexpensive but highly effective method of screening the sleeping area without any loss of light.*

◁ **❷ HEARTH AND HOME**
A gas coal-effect fire, cushions, and shelves crammed with books and other treasured possessions create an inviting and homely focus to the living area.

**❸ WEST-FACING WINDOW** ▷
The west-facing end wall is entirely glazed, filling the apartment with light for the best part of the day and giving the illusion of the interior flowing out to the timber-decked roof terrace. A window-cleaner's ladder provides access to the high-level bed alcove.

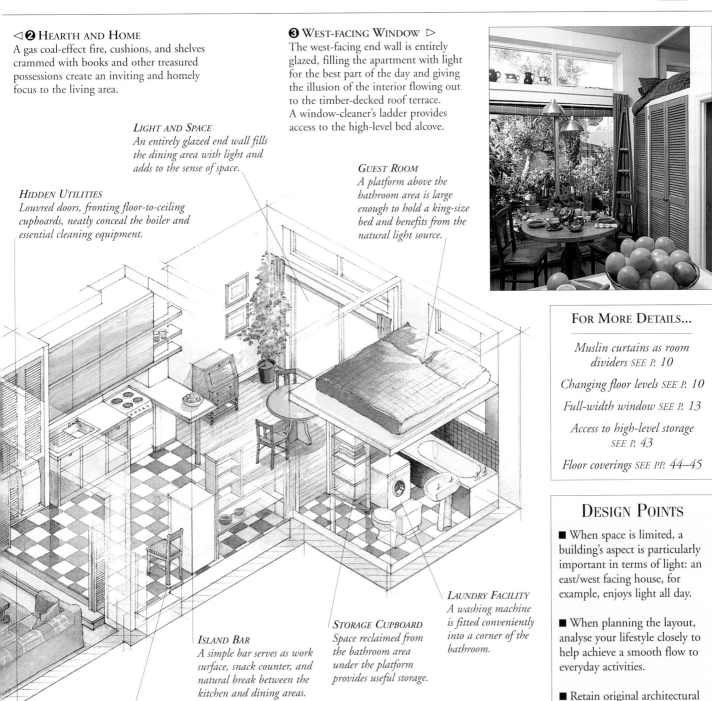

*LIGHT AND SPACE*
An entirely glazed end wall fills the dining area with light and adds to the sense of space.

*GUEST ROOM*
A platform above the bathroom area is large enough to hold a king-size bed and benefits from the natural light source.

*HIDDEN UTILITIES*
Louvred doors, fronting floor-to-ceiling cupboards, neatly conceal the boiler and essential cleaning equipment.

*ISLAND BAR*
A simple bar serves as work surface, snack counter, and natural break between the kitchen and dining areas.

*STORAGE CUPBOARD*
Space reclaimed from the bathroom area under the platform provides useful storage.

*LAUNDRY FACILITY*
A washing machine is fitted conveniently into a corner of the bathroom.

*ENTRANCE*
The only entrance to the apartment leads directly into the kitchen area from the communal hallway of the building.

*CHANGING LEVELS*
The raised kitchen floor level physically separates the cooking and living spaces.

**❹ UNINTERRUPTED SPACE** ▷
For those living in one room, linear interior space has the practical advantage of permitting easy, unimpeded movement. Equally importantly, a long view through to a garden or roof terrace helps to dispel any feelings of claustrophobia that may be created by living in a confined area.

## FOR MORE DETAILS...

*Muslin curtains as room dividers* SEE P. 10

*Changing floor levels* SEE P. 10

*Full-width window* SEE P. 13

*Access to high-level storage* SEE P. 43

*Floor coverings* SEE PP. 44–45

## DESIGN POINTS

■ When space is limited, a building's aspect is particularly important in terms of light: an east/west facing house, for example, enjoys light all day.

■ When planning the layout, analyse your lifestyle closely to help achieve a smooth flow to everyday activities.

■ Retain original architectural features and incorporate them into your plan. For example, you may consider filling the alcoves on either side of a chimney breast with shelving.

■ Don't waste space, no matter how small, oddly shaped, or unconventional. The most unlikely places can usually hold items for storage.

■ Position a sleeping platform near a top-opening window so that the area has its own source of natural light and ventilation.

# LINEAR ROOM CHOICE

### △ UNIFIED SPACE
Although the separate sleeping, cooking, and dining areas in this restricted living space are divided by cupboards, shelves, and a solid wall, the white paintwork and single type of flooring throughout help to unify the interior and prevent any feelings of claustrophobia.

### SPACE AND LIGHT ▷
The double-height window, towards which the living and sleeping areas are oriented, links the interior with the exterior, bathing the former with light. White paint, upholstery, and linen help to reflect the light around the apartment and enhance the feeling of free-flowing space, which is unimpeded by screens or partitions.

### △ ROOM IN A GARDEN
The entire end wall of the kitchen area has been transformed into a glazed conservatory, cleverly integrating the garden and the interior, while a curved island worktop with inset sink and drainer takes advantage of the natural light and panoramic garden view to create a pleasant workplace.

### △ DEFINING SPACE
Semi-transparent materials add an interesting texture to walls and dividers. As well as acting as a screen and creating a sense of privacy, they permit light to be filtered through and draw the eye to the space beyond. In this interior, rugs laid at right angles also help to define different areas.

### △ DIVIDING A LARGE SPACE
The scale of this former industrial interior could be overwhelming but, by placing a sofa against a panelled wall at right angles to the dining area and installing a bamboo blind to screen off the entrance, comfortable divisions have been created without losing the overall flow of space.

# COMPACT ROOM PLAN

TWO ROOMS ON THE GROUND FLOOR of a city terraced house have been transformed into a studio space that, despite occupying only about 42 square metres (450 square feet), gives an overall impression of light and space. The carefully considered colour treatment of surfaces in the kitchen is enhanced by the otherwise white interior, as are the collections of coloured glassware displayed in the studio.

INTERNAL ROOM DIMENSIONS:
5m (16ft) WIDE
9m (29ft) LONG

*Sleeping platform, with kitchen unit and dining area below*

*Bay window*

*Boiler*

*Washing machine*

*Cooking area*

*Bathroom, with storage area above*

*Hanging rails*

*Stacking wire storage*

*Entrance hall, with storage above*

*Living area*

△ BIRD'S EYE VIEW
Parts of the original dividing wall remain, but the effect is of a single space, with the advantage of natural light from three sides. Although functional areas have been reduced to a minimum, there is no loss of comfort.

## DESIGN POINTS

■ Whenever possible, try to construct a sleeping platform alongside a window to ensure good ventilation and a source of natural light.

■ Even in a very small living area, it should be possible to find space to display collections of objects; look especially at any tall, narrow gaps.

■ A simple worktop and a pair of folding or stacking trestles provide a worksurface or a dining table for entertaining guests, and can be stored unobtrusively until required.

■ Check with an architect on fixed structural features, then look for imaginative ways of incorporating them into your overall plan.

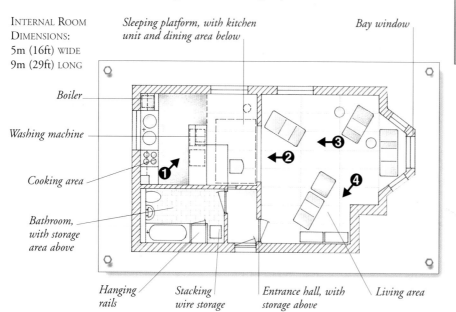

△ ❶ PLATFORM ABOVE THE KITCHEN
The ceiling is about 3 metres (10 feet) high, allowing for a sleeping platform large enough to hold a television and books by the bed. Natural light and ventilation are provided by a window shared with the area below.

*SHARED WINDOW*
*One window is shared between the living area below and the sleeping platform above.*

*CONCEALED BOILER*
*The boiler is fitted into a corner behind a white cupboard front.*

*SPACE-SAVING LADDER*
*Sturdy rungs, originally from a ships' chandler, provide access to the sleeping platform.*

*PURPOSE-BUILT UNIT*
*A washing machine, microwave, fridge, and vegetable rack are all housed in a purpose-built unit.*

◁ ❷ OCCASIONAL DINING FURNITURE
When a dining space is needed, the worksurface is folded away and a dining table assembled from a simple table-top and trestles, which are easily stored, along with the stacking chairs, when not in use. The flat, painted kitchen unit conceals a fridge, washing machine and microwave oven.

*VERTICAL LIGHTING*
*A 1970s Italian lamp runs on a cable from ceiling to floor, through a hole in the platform.*

*WINDOW FEATURE*
*Original large bay window provides natural light that is reflected throughout the interior.*

*MODULAR SEATING*
*Foam seating units interlock to double as a spare bed when required.*

△ ❸ INSTANT WORKSTATION
A simple workstation is quickly assembled by lifting the horizontally hinged table-top and supporting it on another panel, which is hung vertically. When not in use, the panels fold unobtrusively against the kitchen unit, which not only provides a useful shelf, but also screens off much of the cooking area.

---

FOR MORE DETAILS...

*Modular foam furniture*
SEE P. *20*

*Stacking chairs* SEE P. *29*

*Hinged workstation*
SEE PP. *30–31*

---

*FLEXIBLE SHELVING*
*A modular shelving system, packed with books, CDs, and audio equipment, can be added to as necessary.*

*STORAGE SPACE*
*A hatch leads to storage space above the entrance lobby and bathroom.*

*ENTRANCE LOBBY*
*Access to the apartment from the communal hallway is via a lobby, which also houses shoe storage.*

*MINIMAL WARDROBE*
*Two hanging rails, one above the other, and a mobile stack of wire baskets constitute the wardrobe.*

*COMPACT BATHROOM*
*The bathroom has just enough room for a bath with fitted shower, WC, and handbasin.*

△ ❹ MODULAR STORAGE RACK
Storage of books, magazines, telephone/fax machine, and mini sound system is all contained within a modular metal rack system along one wall.

# COMPACT ROOM CHOICE

## △ KITCHEN IN A CUPBOARD

An imaginative variation on the kitchen-in-a-cupboard theme is to recycle a secondhand wardrobe. Here, a small sink has been plumbed in, with shelving and drawers underneath. Tiling and shelves complete this neat, hide-away unit.

## △ REMODELLED ROOM

A deep, false wall provides a practical way of creating a room within a room. Here, above a large amount of storage space and a doorway, a spacious bedroom has been created, the whole structure lightened by being painted completely white.

## △ CORNER KITCHEN

A compact kitchen, with a sink, small hob, and extractor fan, has been fitted into this corner, with suspended shelving above.

## COLOUR COORDINATION ▷

Many space-creating features, such as a convertible sofa-bed, folding chairs, and a glass-topped table, are demonstrated in this small studio, which also illustrates the way in which colour can be used to enhance the sense of space.

# OPEN-PLAN ROOM PLAN

METICULOUS PLANNING along strong horizontal axes gives this studio, which measures only 5 x 8.5 metres (17 x 28 feet), a feeling of calm spaciousness despite its busy urban location. The functional areas are defined by varying floor levels and by boxed-in vertical supports, but the horizontal flow of space is maintained, with no view being blocked by a full-height wall.

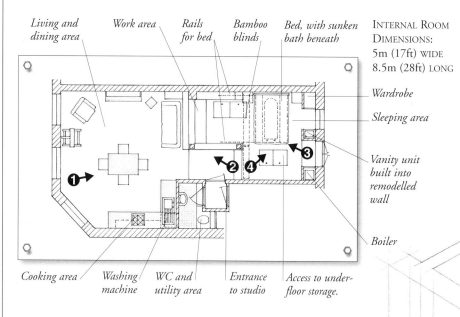

Living and dining area
Work area
Rails for bed
Bamboo blinds
Bed, with sunken bath beneath

INTERNAL ROOM DIMENSIONS:
5m (17ft) WIDE
8.5m (28ft) LONG

Wardrobe

Sleeping area

Vanity unit built into remodelled wall

Boiler

Cooking area
Washing machine
WC and utility area
Entrance to studio
Access to under-floor storage.

### FOR MORE DETAILS...

Bath under bed SEE PP. 32–33

Fold-away ironing table SEE P. 37

Underfloor storage SEE P. 42

△ BIRD'S EYE VIEW
A vast amount of concealed storage space has been planned into this studio, as well as an ingenious, double-function sleeping and washing area.

*DUAL-PURPOSE TABLE-TOP*
A folded table-top extension, which fits over the dining table, makes up the front of this storage cupboard.

*ARTISTIC FOCUS*
An artist's easel provides a clue to the interests enjoyed by the occupant of this serene studio.

◁❶ UNBROKEN VIEW
The dining area is located at the junction of the two major axes, accentuating the length of the interior. Since no solid wall interrupts the view, the sitting, working, cooking, and sleeping areas are all visible.

*FLEXIBLE SEATING*
When not in use, these lightweight folding metal chairs with wooden slats can be easily stored.

◁ ❷ RAISED WORKSTATION
The centrally placed work area is on a raised
level that not only separates it from the living
and dining areas, but also provides extensive
underfloor storage space.

*UNDERBED STORAGE*
*Although the bed*
*contains large, built-*
*in storage drawers, it*
*can be easily rolled*
*over the sunken bath.*

*SCREENING OPTIONS*
*Two bamboo blinds screen off either*
*the sleeping/washing area or the*
*entire end section of the studio.*

*STUDY AREA*
*A large bookshelf*
*along the side wall*
*emphasizes the*
*horizontal*
*accent.*

*VANITY UNIT*
*A small basin and*
*cupboard are concealed*
*in the remodelled*
*end wall.*

△ ❸ HORIZONTAL AXES
The interior of the apartment is illuminated by
reflected light from windows at both ends of the
room, although privacy in the bathing and sleeping
area can be created by lowering the bamboo blinds.

*CONCEALED BOILER*
*Hidden in the remodelled*
*wall is a combination boiler,*
*which obviates the need for*
*a bulky hot water tank.*

*UNDERFLOOR STORAGE*
*Marine-style hatches give*
*access to long-term storage*
*space beneath the raised*
*timber flooring.*

*BUILT-IN TOOL CHEST*
*The stair-tread lifts up to*
*reveal additional storage*
*space that is ideal for tools.*

*DEAD SPACE*
*A washing machine, accessed*
*from the toilet/utility room,*
*fills the otherwise inaccessible*
*space in the kitchen unit.*

## DESIGN POINTS

■ Create a sense of warmth
and cohesion in an open-plan
interior by choosing natural
materials such as wood,
bamboo, and plain cotton.

■ Forget tradition when fitting
plumbed-in equipment: it may
be cheaper to take the machine
to the plumbing rather than
the plumbing to the machine.

■ To increase a sense of space
and avoid claustrophobia, limit
dividing walls to half height.

■ Vary floor levels to create
spatial variety and to provide
underfloor storage space.

■ Avoid condensation in a
windowless internal bath area
by fitting an extractor fan.

*FOLD-AWAY IRONING BOARD*
*An extending ironing board*
*occupies minimal space in the*
*fitted kitchen unit.*

❹ JAPANESE-STYLE BATHROOM ▷
A spacious bathroom is created by lowering the
blinds and rolling back the bed to reveal the
sunken bath. The remodelled end wall contains
a wardrobe, cupboards, and vanity unit.

# Open-plan Room choice

### △ Half-wall Divider
The upstand at the back of this kitchen worktop successfully separates the preparation and cooking areas from the main living space, without blocking them off entirely.

### ◁ Underfloor Storage
Constructing a new, raised floor level is a way of creating a room within a room, as well as providing a large amount of useful and easily accessible long-term storage space.

### △ Space-defining Devices
Functional areas are defined here by devices such as blinds, half-height walls, and different floor levels. The bathroom is visually separated, with minimal privacy, but remains part of the main living area.

### High-level Reading Area ▷
If ceiling height permits, the construction of a gallery releases living space. Here, a library above a bank of roomy cupboards has been created. Painted white, they merge successfully into the general structure.

# LARGE ROOM PLAN

WITH THE ORIGINAL TILING RESTORED and the aggregate pillars and ducting left exposed, the industrial aesthetic is retained in this loft in a converted riverside warehouse. The effect is softened, however, by the use of colour and the introduction of antique furniture. As the ceiling is not high enough to construct another floor, a galleried work area has been created above a bank of built-in kitchen cupboards.

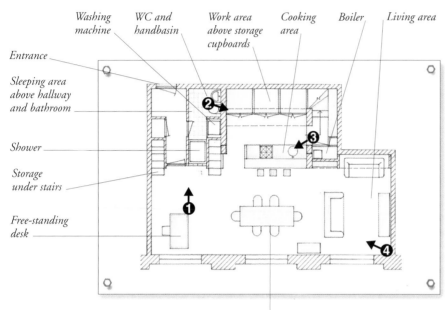

Washing machine · WC and handbasin · Work area above storage cupboards · Cooking area · Boiler · Living area

Entrance

Sleeping area above hallway and bathroom

Shower

Storage under stairs

Free-standing desk

Dining area

**BIRD'S EYE VIEW** △
Three large windows, providing a view of the river and a source of natural light, are a major feature in this loft and formed the main influence on the plan, which packs all services against the inner wall.

INTERNAL ROOM
DIMENSIONS:
7m (24ft) WIDE
11m (36ft) LONG

*FITTED WARDROBE*
Along the back wall, a fitted wardrobe and cupboards are painted a cheery bright yellow.

*PLATFORM BED*
The bed is sunk into the platform and surrounded by a wide ledge.

*ENTRANCE HALL*
The door to the loft is under the deep platform, creating a dramatic entrance.

*BELOW-STAIRS STORAGE*
In the entrance hall, under the stairs, is a space for coats and cleaning equipment.

*SHOWER CUBICLE*
Alongside the utility area is a large shower with natural light transmitted through glass bricks.

### FOR MORE DETAILS...

*Workstation with glazed panels SEE P. 11*

*Glass brick panel in internal shower-room SEE P. 12*

*Built-in shelves lining entire wall SEE P. 42–43*

◁ ❶ **COLOURFUL ENTRANCE**
Above the entrance to the loft is a symmetrically planned sleeping platform with built-in wardrobes behind. The bathroom, utility area, and shower cubicle are underneath, with natural light entering through the glass brick wall. Two sets of deep steps conceal long-term storage.

◁ ❷ HIGH-LEVEL WORKSTATION
The long work desk, which has been built
on a raised platform above the walk-in
kitchen cupboards, offers an overall view
of the loft interior and of the river, as well
as providing a quiet work space that is
separate yet still part of the whole.

❸ DUAL-PURPOSE BREAKFAST BAR ▷
The food preparation and washing-up
areas are screened by an oak upstand that
functions as both a breakfast bar and a
space divider. The bar is fitted with small
strip lights that give a decorative effect as
well as useful illumination.

*WALL OF STORAGE*
*Bookshelves, holding magazines, books,*
*and storage boxes, have been fitted into*
*one entire wall of the loft.*

*EXTRA LIGHT*
*Sandblasted glazing*
*panels along the lower*
*front of the desk allow*
*light into the darkest*
*part of the work*
*platform.*

*INDOOR GARDEN*
*A shelf of plants*
*introduces a natural*
*detail to the industrial*
*scale of the loft space.*

*WALK-IN LARDERS*
*Capacious walk-in cupboards*
*contain a microwave and*
*freezer as well as other*
*kitchen equipment and food.*

*OLD AND NEW*
*A large renovated*
*antique wardrobe*
*adds a personal touch.*

## DESIGN POINTS

■ When planning a loft space,
aim to work with, not against,
the existing structure and, if
possible, try to accommodate
the existing services.

■ Opt for glass bricks instead
of a solid wall to allow light
into a dark interior space while
still preserving privacy.

■ If you work from home, try
to separate the work space from
the main living area.

■ Sensitively handled colour is
a useful device for defining
function, shaping space, and
providing a focus.

■ Salvaged or antique furniture
adds individuality to an
industrial-scale interior.

*OAK WORKTOP AND COUNTER*
*All the kitchen appliances are built-*
*in behind the worktop and counter,*
*which are made of oak – the same*
*wood as the flooring.*

❹ COLOUR-CODED AREAS ▷
With the different living zones clearly colour-
coded – blue for the bathroom, yellow for the
sleeping and work spaces, and salmon-pink
for the kitchen and living areas – the effect is
reminiscent of an abstract Cubist interior.

*ANTIQUE DESK*
*An antique "partners' desk", at*
*right angles to the dining table,*
*commands a long view of the loft.*

# LARGE ROOM CHOICE

△ DISTINCTIVE FEATURE
A sense of scale has been given to the interior by this dramatic roof truss – an original architectural feature that has been retained and incorporated into the shelves and worktop. The kitchen area is defined by studded rubber flooring and screened by a sliding door that becomes part of a wall of cupboards when closed.

△ FULL-HEIGHT SCREEN
Painted in a strong colour, against which red and white furniture and a collection of ceramics stand out in contrast, a blank, full-height wall screens off the kitchen area while still allowing a flow of air and space. A small painting provides a focus.

◁ SCULPTURED LIVING
In this minimalist interior, living elements – contained along one side of the loft behind blocks of fitted storage – are reduced to abstract sculptural forms. The use of soft colour and a natural timber flooring averts any impression of coldness.

CREATED LIGHT AND SPACE ▷
Although this corner kitchen has no natural light source, a sense of light and spaciousness has been achieved. A glass shelf with a stainless steel hanging rail is suspended above the island bar, with additional glass and metal fixtures along the rear wall. Colour has been used to define a large flat expanse of architrave.

# GALLERIED ROOM PLAN

A SHELL-AND-CORE CONVERSION in part of a redeveloped warehouse, this space, measuring 53 square metres (570 square feet), has been fitted out by architects specializing in loft design. The use of strong colours softens the industrial rawness of exposed ducting and brickwork, and only the bed deck, floating dramatically above the kitchen/dining section, breaks the curve of the wall containing the functional areas.

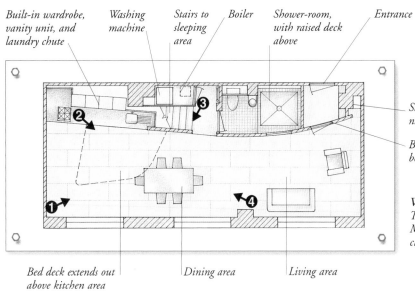

Built-in wardrobe, vanity unit, and laundry chute

Washing machine

Stairs to sleeping area

Boiler

Shower-room, with raised deck above

Entrance

Shelves in narrow alcove

Built-in functional areas behind curved wall

Bed deck extends out above kitchen area

Dining area

Living area

### BIRD'S EYE VIEW △
All the service elements are tucked away behind the curved wall, leaving a clear living space that has the benefit of natural light from three windows.

INTERNAL ROOM DIMENSIONS:
4.6m (15ft) WIDE
11.6m (38ft) LONG

### BED-DECK ILLUMINATION
Halogen lamps are clamped at low levels to the balustrade surrounding the bed deck.

### WALL OF STORAGE
The built-in storage unit, made of MDF, has a space-saving, pull-out clothes rail and shoe shelves.

### FOR MORE DETAILS...

*Cooking area with suspended glass cooker hood* SEE P. 26

*Shower-room* SEE P. 32

*Built-in wardrobe* SEE P. 42
*Vertical ladder made from scaffold sections* SEE P. 43

### ◁ ❶ SPACIOUS LINES
A continuous, uncluttered stretch of birch-faced ply flooring follows the elegant line of the service wall, whose double height makes the living space appear larger than it is. The loft height is also accentuated by light reflected onto the main end wall from concealed strip lighting in a narrow alcove.

### EXTRACTOR HOOD
Above the hob, a suspended sheet of etched glass provides an unusual and attractive hood for the extractor ducting.

### NATURAL MATERIAL
A slate worktop, with integral grooved draining board, is fitted over the kitchen units.

## ◁ ❷ OVERALL VIEWS

This is a loft with exciting perspectives in all directions: from the bed deck, beyond the wall-mounted television, the main loft space is visible, while the second deck, with shower-room below, can be seen to the left.

**SECONDARY DECK**
*A raised deck above the shower-room can be used as a guest room or for storage.*

**CLOTHES-CARE SOLUTION**
*Leading to the utility area and washing machine below is a useful laundry chute.*

**VERTICAL LADDER**
*Access to the raised deck is constructed from scaffold sections.*

## ❸ CONTRASTING FEATURES ▷

Behind the facade, the warm, colourful sleeping area, reached by narrow steps, provides a contrast to the expanse of raw brickwork and large-scale original windows in this industrial space.

**PERFORATED METAL SCREEN**
*A panel of perforated metal, spot-lit from behind and floating proud of the wall, allows light into the deck area.*

**NATURAL LIGHT**
*Light filters into the bathroom through a frosted glass window.*

**REFLECTED LIGHTING**
*Light from the strip lighting behind these narrow vertical shelves is reflected back into the main living area.*

## DESIGN POINTS

■ It is possible to fit all the functional areas into a tight plan, as long as the living area maintains a free flow of space.

■ Colour plays an important part in shaping an interior: a cool, minimalist, industrial-style loft can be humanized by an expanse of strong colour.

■ A wardrobe with short, pull-out hanging rails can be fitted into a shallower space than one with a single end-to-end rail.

**LUXURY SHOWER-ROOM**
*Although wide enough for a bath, the area is fitted with a stainless steel shower tray and an extra-large shower head.*

## ❹ SLEEPING BALCONY ▷

Perched on an exposed steel beam above the kitchen area is a bed deck with a balustrade of perforated aluminium. It appears like a theatre balcony, lit by mini halogen lamps, yet the deck provides a comfortable sleeping platform with built-in storage alongside.

**SERVICE PANELS**
*Access to lighting transformers under the bed deck is provided by removable panels.*

# Galleried Room choice

△ **Vertical Access**
The industrial impression of a steel ladder leading up to the sleeping platform in this loft apartment is softened by the lavender paintwork.

◁ **Natural Choice**
Bamboo blinds, basketware, wood fittings, and a soft carpet provide warm natural colours and textures that harmonize with the exposed brick walls and ceiling beams.

△ **Corner Kitchen**
A mini kitchen has been neatly slotted into the corner beneath the narrow gallery. Boldly painted sliding doors allow the paraphernalia of plumbing, ducts, and kitchen storage to be quickly concealed from view.

**Rustic Charm** ▷
This homely kitchen, brightened by natural light, fits neatly under a wide gallery. It illustrates the delightful effect that can be achieved by furnishing a kitchen with old items of furniture instead of fitted units.

# LOFT PLAN

THE DISTINGUISHING FEATURE of this minimalist, high-tech loft is the use of remote-controlled, aluminium slatted blinds to divide up the space at different times of the day, while still allowing light to filter through. The device introduces an element of fun and adds to the astonishing illusion of space created by an entire wall of mirror. All the light sources are concealed so that this studio is filled with reflected light.

△ ❷ KITCHEN SCREENING
With the blind lowered and the slats only partially closed, reflections from downlighters play on the polished granite countertop, animating the kitchen area behind.

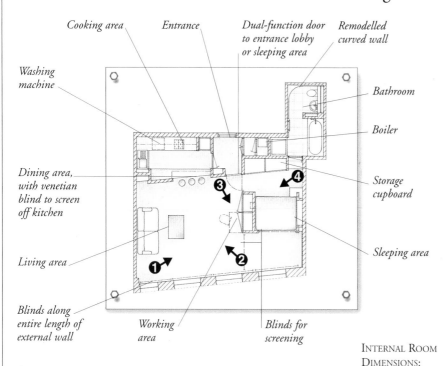

Cooking area
Entrance
Dual-function door to entrance lobby or sleeping area
Remodelled curved wall
Washing machine
Bathroom
Boiler
Dining area, with venetian blind to screen off kitchen
Storage cupboard
Living area
Sleeping area
Blinds along entire length of external wall
Working area
Blinds for screening

△ BIRD'S EYE VIEW
The kitchen, bathroom, and storage areas are sited along the internal wall, while the uncluttered, main living space of the loft enjoys the natural light flowing in from the large windows.

INTERNAL ROOM DIMENSIONS:
6.7m (22ft) WIDE
8.1m (26ft) LONG

## DESIGN POINTS

■ A sequence of blinds can dramatically alter an interior space, creating new areas and separating off others.

■ Mirror is a powerful source of illusion. The larger it is, the more effective, but even a small framed mirror can give the impression of a room beyond.

■ Balance the cool effect of a minimalist, high-tech loft with the warmth of a timber floor. Parquet laid at right angles to the main axis will appear to widen an interior space.

ALCOVE SHELVING
Shelving is tucked into a corner alcove, below a lowered ceiling with concealed lighting.

BREAKFAST BAR
A polished granite worktop provides a dining bar between the kitchen and the living area.

◁ ❶ SHIMMERING REFLECTIVE WALL
The entire external wall of the loft is fitted with aluminium blinds. These create a shimmering wall that is reflected in the mirrored end wall, visually doubling the space. A bright red table adds a splash of colour to this cool interior.

**KITCHEN BLIND**
*A blind screens off the entire kitchen and dining space.*

**CURVED WALL**
*A gently curving false wall leads you round into the lavatory area.*

❸ **INSTANT OFFICE** ▷
A small home office is quickly assembled out of the bank of storage by opening one cupboard door as a gate-leg support and dropping down another as a work surface.

**DUAL-FUNCTION DOOR**
*The entrance door can be used to close off access to the bedroom and bathroom.*

**STORAGE BANK**
*A bank of cupboards provides generous storage space and screens the sleeping area.*

**BEDSIDE STORAGE**
*A useful set of narrow shelves is concealed at either side of the bedhead.*

**CREATING SPACE**
*Remote-controlled venetian blinds screen off the bed and create a private or spare bedroom area alongside.*

**MIRROR ILLUSION**
*An end wall completely filled with mirror visually doubles the length of the studio and increases the light level.*

## FOR MORE DETAILS...

*Curved bathroom wall*
SEE P. *13*

*Mirrored wall* SEE P. *13*

*Granite breakfast bar*
SEE PP. *28–29*

*Blinds as screens* SEE P. *38*

**FOLD-DOWN DESK**
*A useful home office space, created out of two cupboard fronts, is hidden from view when not in use.*

❹ **PRIVATE SLEEPING AREA** ▷
The bed, with storage drawer underneath, is shielded by a bank of cupboards featuring a small, square, Japanese-style display cavity. By lowering a blind on the left-hand side, and swinging round the entrance door to close off the other side, a private sleeping area is created.

**WALL OF BLINDS**
*Remote-controlled aluminium venetian blinds, covering four windows, line the entire external wall of the loft.*

# LOFT CHOICE

◁ TOWEL-RAIL ROOM DIVIDER
Decorative in shape, colour, and
finish, towel radiators are no longer
merely functional items, but play an
important role in bathroom design.
A free-standing vertical panel or
ladder-style radiator, for example,
can act not just as a towel rail and
room heater but also as a room
divider in an open-plan loft space.

DIVIDING LOFT SPACE ▷
Several ways of dividing space are
illustrated in this minimalist loft.
Extra-wide folding panels can be
rapidly pulled across to conceal the
kitchen, which is built under a
gallery that divides the vertical space
at one end of the room. A panel of
translucent glazing allows light into
a private area of the gallery, while a
curved metal balustrade partially
screens the open section.

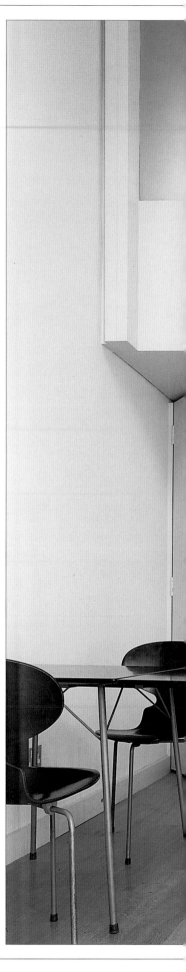

△ INDUSTRIAL SLIDING PANELS
Suspended, factory-style sliding panels offer a
high-tech alternative to folding doors and blinds
for screening off areas within a room. They take
up less space than any folding system and can be
faced with a choice of finishes, from metallic
laminate to cork, paint, and plastics.

△ PART-GLAZED SCREEN
A quiet home-working space has been created
here by placing a solid white screen behind the
sofa. Above the screen is a glazed panel that
allows the light and the line of the flush wall
cupboards to flow through, following the
direction of the flooring planks.

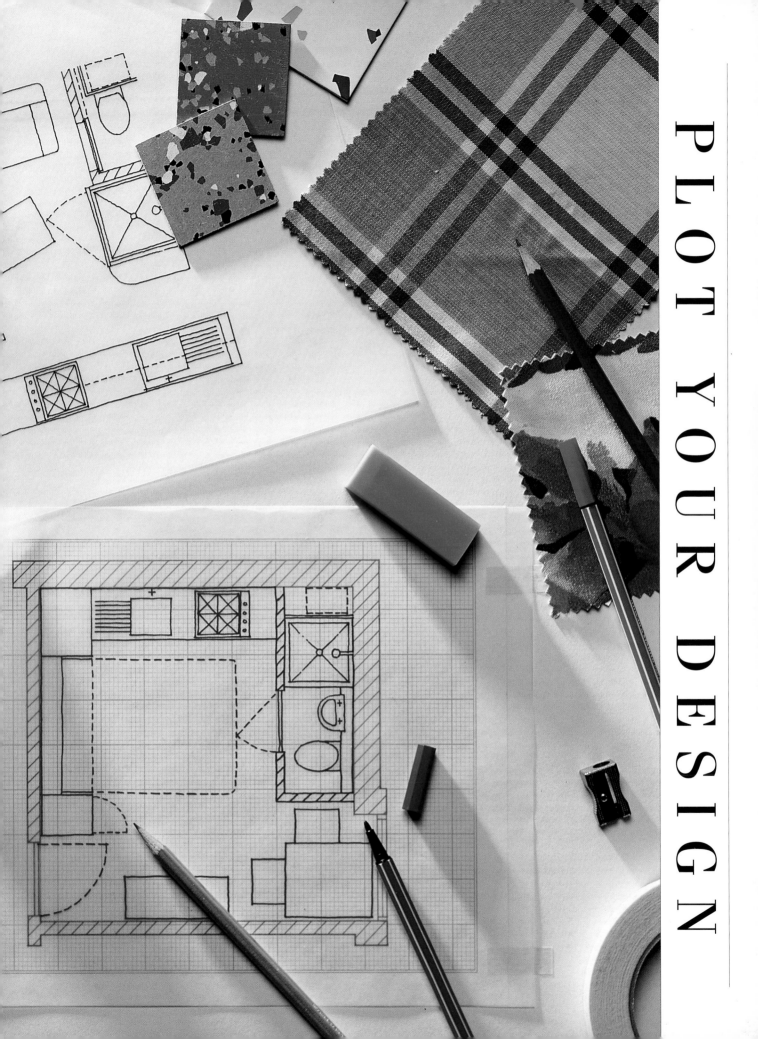

PLOT YOUR DESIGN

# PLOT YOUR ROOM

THE FIRST STEP IN PLANNING is to make a careful survey of your existing room so that accurate scale drawings of the floor plan and elevations can be produced. It is useful to take a series of reference photographs of the room at this stage.

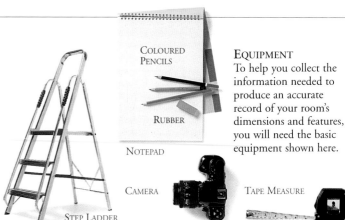

COLOURED PENCILS

RUBBER

NOTEPAD

**EQUIPMENT**
To help you collect the information needed to produce an accurate record of your room's dimensions and features, you will need the basic equipment shown here.

STEP LADDER

CAMERA

TAPE MEASURE

## FLOOR DIMENSIONS

You do not need to be an architect to draw an accurate plan, but only accurate measurements can tell you if existing appliances and furniture will fit in your new space. Familiarize yourself with the interior, especially details such as the location of services, any changes in floor level, and load-bearing features that cannot be altered. Although professional help may be needed to deal with these (especially if service points have to be moved), try to begin visualizing the room as your future living space.

**❶ DRAW A FLOOR PLAN**
The first step in producing a floor plan is simply to draw a rough sketch of the floor area, making sure that you include features such as chimney breasts, alcoves, and any fixed furniture that you plan to incorporate into your new design.

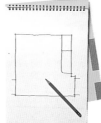

**❷ MEASURE THE FLOOR**
Next, measure the length and breadth of the floor and note the measurements on your sketch. It may be worth checking the measurements at different points, as walls are not always square. Note also the measurement of any alcoves or other features.

**❸ PLOT WALL LENGTHS**
Working round the room, measure the length of each wall, carefully noting down the measurements on your sketch for future reference. You may find that the room is not symmetrical, and it is useful to know this in advance.

**❹ NOTE SERVICE POINTS**
Survey the room for service points, such as gas supply, electrical sockets, and radiators, and plot their position on your sketch. Indicate structural features such as chimney flues and outside walls, and make a note of room orientation.

**❺ PLOT FIXED FIXTURES**
Measure the dimensions of any built-in cupboards or shelving that you wish to retain, noting their position in the room, and adding them to your sketch. It may be quite straightforward, however, to relocate such items if you wish.

**❻ PHOTOGRAPH ODD CORNERS**
Take reference photographs to help you record areas of the room that are difficult to measure, such as awkward corners or sloping walls. Photographs of certain features will help you to recall style details when you start designing your new room.

# WALL ELEVATIONS

Detailed elevations are not necessary, but a sketch survey of all walls is useful, especially if the ceiling is high enough to allow a gallery or platform bed to be constructed. These sketches will help to establish whether there is enough wall space for furniture, without blocking windows, radiators, or other fixed features. Elevations help you to imagine how your space will be when furnished.

**❶ MEASURE THE HEIGHT**
Stand facing each wall in turn and draw a rough sketch. Draw in doors, windows, and alcoves. Now measure the floor-to-ceiling height and note this on the sketch. Architectural features, such as mouldings, are not important at this stage.

**❷ MEASURE THE DOORS**
On each wall sketch, record the height and width of any doors, skirting boards, and cornices, plus details of any frames or mouldings. Note which way the doors are hung and the position of any service points that you do not wish to obstruct.

# DRAWING-UP SCALE PLANS

Having made rough sketches, marked with accurate measurements, of your existing space (*see left*), the next step is to draw up the scale plan and elevations on graph paper, with each square representing a set dimension. Then you can start experimenting with ideas for a multi-purpose living space.

*OUTSIDE WALLS*
*Indicate outside walls with a thick border of cross-hatching.*

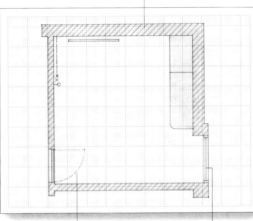

*DOOR OPENING*
*Draw a dotted line to indicate the direction in which the door opens.*

**❷ DRAW UP AN ELEVATION ▷**
Referring to your rough plan for measurements, draw up one wall to scale. Work from the floor upwards, marking on details and services last.

*DOOR HANDLE*
*Indicate the way the door opens by drawing in the door handle.*

**❸ OTHER ELEVATIONS ▽**
Draw each of the remaining elevations to scale, marking on relevant details to give you a complete picture of the room before you begin the design.

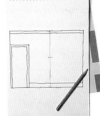

## YOU WILL NEED
Metric and imperial graph paper is supplied with this book, but you will also need a set square, ruler, pen, pencil, pencil sharpener, and rubber.

**◁❶ TRANSFER THE FLOOR PLAN**
Plot the four perimeter walls to scale on graph paper, referring to your rough plan for precise measurements and using a set square to draw right angles. Next, plot key features such as outside walls, doors, windows, and any changes in floor level that are important for planning your space.

*LIGHT*
*Parallel lines show a window as a light source.*

*CORNICE DIMENSIONS*
*The height of storage units will be limited by cornice size.*

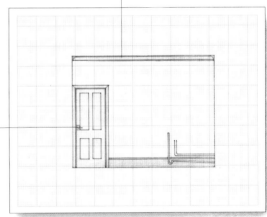

*WINDOWS*
*Include details, such as moulding and windowsill measurements.*

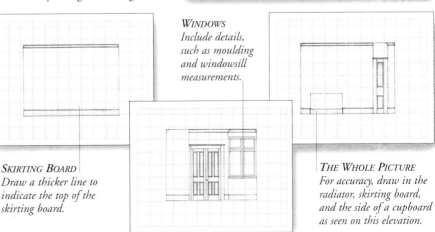

*SKIRTING BOARD*
*Draw a thicker line to indicate the top of the skirting board.*

*THE WHOLE PICTURE*
*For accuracy, draw in the radiator, skirting board, and the side of a cupboard as seen on this elevation.*

# PLACE THE FEATURES

BEGIN BY COMPILING A LIST of all the furniture, appliances, and materials that you wish to include in your room, noting your preferences for where and how you like to eat, work, relax, wash, and sleep. Add to this any special hobby or storage requirements, and then you are ready to find out if your ideal living plan is possible. Place a sheet of tracing paper over the scaled-up room plan and start drawing in the basic fixtures and fittings, bearing in mind our Design Guidelines *(see right)*. You will probably draw many versions and discover unexpected possibilities before reaching the best solution.

TRACING PAPER

SET SQUARE

MASKING TAPE

PEN
SHARPENER
PENCIL
RUBBER

RULER

**YOU WILL NEED ▷**
Place a sheet of tracing paper over your floor plan scale drawing, holding them securely in position with masking tape. Using a soft pencil, ruler, and set square, draw in your listed features in possible locations. Start each new design on a clean sheet of tracing paper.

## DESIGN GUIDELINES

All the elements for one-room living need to be considered together. When planning your space, bear the following points in mind.

❶ CREATE SPACE by careful analysis of requirements, and clever planning, and through the use of multi-purpose furniture, and mobile or folding units.

❷ MAXIMIZE LIGHT by preserving and increasing any sources of natural light with the installation of full-height or full-width mirrors, and by enlarging windows.

❸ USE VERTICAL HEIGHT to create a raised sleeping or working platform, providing a useful storage space underneath.

❹ REDUCE CLUTTER by careful planning of plumbing and electrical services, aiming to box them in as much as possible.

❺ EASE OF ACCESS is essential, so make sure that you leave enough space for doors to open and for unimpeded movement around the furniture and fittings.

## REJECTED PLANS

The complexity of planning for studio living varies according to how much space is available. If the room is large, each living function can be comfortably separated; if it is very small, the aim must be not simply to fit everything in, but to do so in a way that conveys an impression of spaciousness.

**POOR USE OF SPACE ▽**
The cooking area is in the darkest part of the room, with very little worktop space, and the table, seating only two, is in the opposite corner. There is no room for easy chairs.

**BATHROOM DOOR**
*When the bed is down, there is barely room to open the bathroom door.*

**SHOWER AND BOILER**
*The shower cubicle blocks access to the boiler, and their close proximity is potentially hazardous.*

**BLOCKED DOORWAYS ▽**
The futon offers comfortable seating but, when it is opened out, access to the bathroom is blocked. The wardrobe door cannot be fully opened, as the kitchen unit is too close.

**WARDROBE**
*Insufficient room between wardrobe and kitchen unit impedes access.*

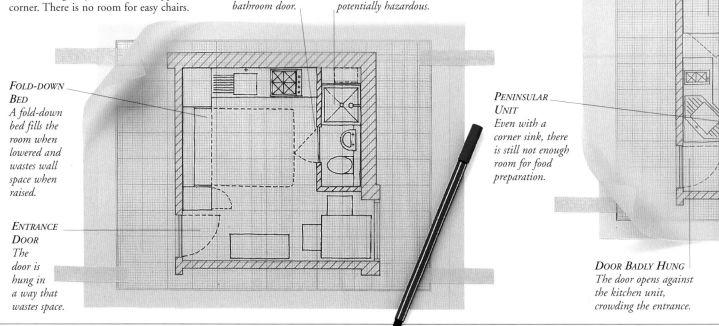

**FOLD-DOWN BED**
*A fold-down bed fills the room when lowered and wastes wall space when raised.*

**ENTRANCE DOOR**
*The door is hung in a way that wastes space.*

**PENINSULAR UNIT**
*Even with a corner sink, there is still not enough room for food preparation.*

**DOOR BADLY HUNG**
*The door opens against the kitchen unit, crowding the entrance.*

# SUCCESSFUL PLAN

With clever planning, and despite limited room, the basic elements for one-room living can be arranged to create a workable space which is neither cramped nor uncomfortable.

**HANDBASIN**
*A mini handbasin has been recessed into the wall of the shower area.*

**BATHROOM DOOR**
*To save space, a sliding door, with a glazed panel to let in light, has been fitted.*

**TWO-RING HOB**
*A practical two-ring hob, built in to the kitchen worktop, provides adequate cooking facilities.*

**BOILER**
*The boiler, behind easily removable shelves, can now be accessed for servicing.*

**MIRROR-FRONTED CUPBOARDS**
*An illusion of space is created in the bathroom by light reflected from the mirrored cupboards.*

**WALL OF STORAGE**
*Every inch of wall space is occupied by cupboards or shelves, which, in turn, can be filled with boxes and files.*

**NARROW WARDROBE**
*A narrow, full-height wardrobe is fitted in between the bathroom and the sofa-bed.*

**DROP-DOWN TABLE**
*A hinged, drop-down table provides a dining table to seat five, or a good-sized work surface.*

**SOFA-BED**
*Maximizing space, the sofa-bed shares space with a drop-down table: when one is down the other is up.*

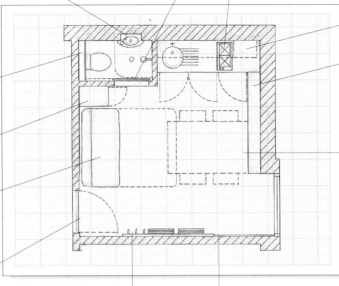

**DOOR REHUNG**
*The door has been rehung, giving a clear entrance and a direct, open view out of the window.*

**SHAKER PEG-RAIL**
*A peg-rail makes the most of wall space for hanging folded chairs, coats, and umbrellas, as well as other hanging storage.*

**FULL-HEIGHT MIRROR**
*Fitted next to the window, a mirror lengthens the interior space and bounces light back into the room.*

◁ **SPACIOUS FEEL**
*A sense of spaciousness has been created by tucking the bathroom into the corner with the plumbing, and making the two major pieces of furniture – the sofa-bed and the table – share the main living area.*

**FUTON**
*The futon provides flexible seating and a bed, but butts up against the kitchen unit when unfolded.*

**POOR ACCESS TO DIFFERENT AREAS** ▽
In this scheme, a studio couch releases space, but this is spoilt by the dominant position of the shower unit, and by the kitchen units blocking light from the only window. There is room for only a low, mobile table for dining purposes.

**CRAMPED TOILET**
*The WC, fitted below the boiler, is cramped, and there is no room for a handbasin.*

**SHOWER CUBICLE**
*A feeling of claustrophobia is created by the too-dominant shower.*

**DINING AREA**
*Wardrobe and bathroom doors open into the centre, leaving room for only a low, mobile table for dining.*

**ACCESS TO BATHROOM**
*With the futon extended, access to the bathroom is blocked. The boiler is still dangerously close.*

**ENTRANCE DOOR**
*The door has been rehung, but the entrance is now visually blocked by kitchen units.*

**BLOCKED WINDOW**
*The only natural light source is partly obscured by kitchen units and corner shelving.*

# PLANNING DETAIL

CHOOSING THE INTERIOR FURNISHINGS AND FINISHES is, for many people, the best part of planning a room. But, when making your choice of furniture, wall coverings, flooring, and lighting, be realistic about your budget and time, as well as bearing in mind our Design Guidelines for studio living (*see p.78*).

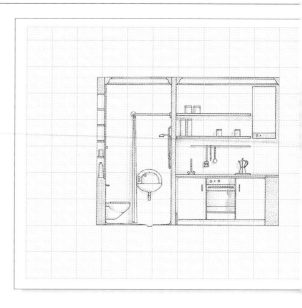

◁ **LIBRARY OF IDEAS**
As part of the planning process, collect pictures from magazines and catalogues that appeal to you, building them up into a library of ideas that will help you to clarify your preferences for furnishing your home.

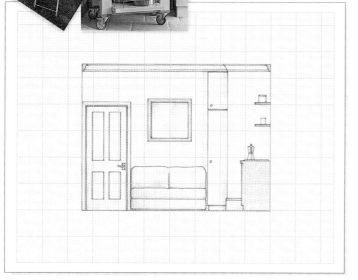

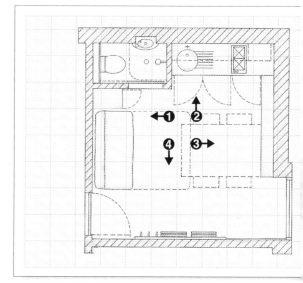

△ ❶ **SLEEPING AND RELAXING AREA**
As there is no room for a bedroom, a sofa-bed provides for both sleeping and relaxing, leaving the central space clear. A floor-to-ceiling wardrobe fills the gap between the sofa-bed and the washing area, while a mirror on the wall above the sofa-bed reflects light from the window opposite.

❹ **USING WALL SPACE** ▷
Space is created by clearing the floor and hanging folding chairs, coats, and umbrellas on a Shaker peg-rail. A full-height mirror alongside the window increases the apparent size of the interior, as well as improving the lighting level in the room.

◁ **COLLECT CATALOGUES**
Send for catalogues of products advertised in magazines, and visit DIY and interior design shops to pick up the latest literature on the furniture and fittings you like.

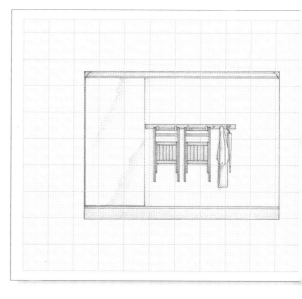

COLOUR SAMPLES ▷
When collecting samples of your favourite materials, colours, and finishes, ask for fairly large pieces: it is hard to visualize the final effect from small samples.

◁ ❷ PLUMBED-IN SERVICES
The bathroom and kitchen have been lined up along one wall with existing plumbing. A curtain can be pulled around the low-level shower to protect the rest of the toilet space, and a mini handbasin is set into the wall. The kitchen has a double hob, oven, utensil rail, and shelving.

## WHAT NEXT?

■ If your plan simply involves moving and fitting ready-made units and appliances, find a recommended joiner or cabinet-maker to help you install these to your design.

■ If you want to move plumbing and wiring, to construct a raised level, or to change the interior structure, contact an architect who will take on the responsibility for dealing with the relevant authorities, obtaining planning permission, and making sure that building regulations are followed.

■ Before starting work, draw up a schedule in conjunction with everybody involved. The usual sequence of events is as follows: structural alterations; wiring and plumbing; floor-laying; cabinet fitting; then final electrical, plumbing, and decoration work.

■ Check that the delivery dates for appliances, cabinets, and materials will meet your agreed work schedule.

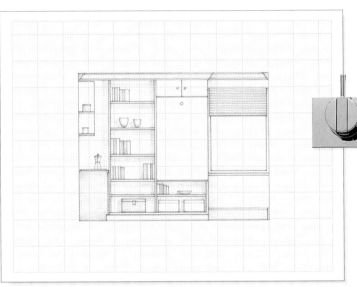

△ FITTINGS
Look for space-saving fittings that combine several functions, such as this immaculately designed one-handle mixer tap with integral soap magnet.

▷ FLOOR PLAN
A bird's eye view of this compact interior shows the elements ranged around the walls, with the sofa-bed and drop-down table sharing the central space.

△ ❸ FITTED STORAGE UNITS
Fitted units are the most efficient way of using space, and help to keep clutter at bay. Behind the drop-down table is a wall of shelves, while the rest of the unit is fitted with more shelves. The traditional casement window has been replaced by a one-pane pivot window for maximum natural light.

FLOORING AND FINISHES ▷
Check the composition when choosing materials. The difference between natural and synthetic materials is now very subtle, and many synthetics offer better and more durable properties than their natural counterparts.

## BUDGET TIPS

■ Once you are satisfied with your initial basic plan, work out the cost of buying the furniture, appliances, fittings, and materials that you have chosen. Obtain estimates from architects, builders, plumbers, electricians, and decorators. If the total cost is beyond your budget, look carefully at each item to see where savings can be made.

■ When costing your design, remember that quality pays when it comes to finishes, both in terms of durability and personal comfort. Beware the false economy of bargains.

# STOCKISTS AND SUPPLIERS

The following directory of companies will help you to find the items that you need for your studio, and to obtain professional advice and information. The letters *(MO)* after an entry indicate that the goods are available by mail order.

## GENERAL

### THE CONRAN SHOP
Michelin House
81 Fulham Road
London SW3 6RD
Tel: 0171 589 7401
*Designer-based contemporary furniture, kitchenware, and accessories.*

### HABITAT (HEAD OFFICE)
196 Tottenham Court Road
London W1P 9LD
Tel: 0171 255 2545 for details of your local branches.
*Folding furniture, mobile storage, modern lighting, and accessories.*

### HEAL'S
196 Tottenham Court Road
London W1P 9LD
Tel: 0171 636 1666
*Stylish contemporary furniture, kitchenware, lighting, and accessories.*

### IKEA LTD
2 Drury Way
255 North Circular Road
London NW10 OJQ
Tel: 0181 233 2300 for details of your local branches.
*Huge selection of modern furniture, storage, lighting, and accessories.*

### THE JOHN LEWIS PARTNERSHIP
278–306 Oxford Street
London W1 1EX
Tel: 0171 629 7711
for local branches.
*Comprehensive range of furniture, domestic equipment, and accessories.*

## FURNITURE AND ACCESSORIES

### AERO WHOLESALE LTD
96 Westbourne Grove
London W2 5RT
Tel: 0171 221 1950
*Contemporary furniture and accessories for the home. (Also available MO)*

### AFTER NOAH
121 Upper Street
London N1 1QP
Tel: 0171 359 4281
*Space-saving furniture and storage solutions. (Also available MO)*

### AZUMI'S
Basement, 7 Holmdale Road
London NW6 1BE
Tel: 0171 435 5398
*Folding and space-saving furniture.*

### CENTURY DESIGN
68 Marylebone High Street
London W1M 3AQ
Tel: 0171 487 5100
*American mid-century design classics.*

### COLOUR BLUE
Beckhaven House
9 Gilbert Road
London SE11 5AA
Tel: 0171 820 7700 for catalogue and details of shops.
*Mediterranean-style furnishings. (MO)*

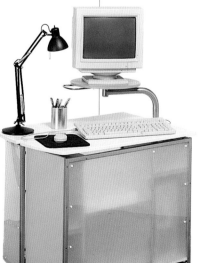

### JONATHAN FIELD
Tel: 0181 809 1593
for details.
*Screenrobe wardrobe/ screens.*

### GRAHAM & GREEN
4–7 & 10 Elgin Crescent
London W11 2JA
Tel: 0171 729 4594
*Folding garden furniture, kitchen equipment, and accessories. (Also available MO).*

### JERRY'S HOME STORE
163–67 Fulham Road
London SW3 6SN
Tel: 0171 225 2246
*American homewares.*

### LIGNE ROSET (UK) LTD
95a High Street
Great Missenden
Bucks HP16 OAL
Tel: 01494 865001 for local stockists.
*Contemporary furniture for modern homes.*

### MUJI
26 Great Marlborough Street
London W1V 1HL
Tel: 0171 494 1197
*Storage, mobile units, and home accessories including futons.*

### NUMBER 48
48 White Hart Lane
London SW13
Tel: 0181 878 6861
*Antiques and decorative items.*

### NICE HOUSE
Unit 8, Italian Centre
Glasgow GH 1HD
Tel: 0141 533 1377
*Design-led furniture, lighting, and accessories. (Also available MO)*

### THE PIER
200 Tottenham Court Road
London W1P OAD
Tel: 0171 637 7001 for details.
*Stacking baskets, folding chairs, and soft hanging wardrobes.*

### PRECIOUS McBANE
11 Clink Street Studios, Soho Wharf
1 Clink Street
London SE1 9TG
Tel: 0171 403 5270
*Couture furniture and accessories, made to commisson.*

### PURVES & PURVES
80–1 & 83 Tottenham Court Road
London W1P 9HD
Tel: 0171 580 8223
*Contemporary furniture and furnishings. (MO; call 01709 889900 for mini catalogue).*

### SCP
135–39 Curtain Road
London EC2
Tel: 0171 739 1869
*Stackable, mobile, modern furniture, including screens and sofabeds.*

### THE SHAKER SHOP
25 Harcourt Street
London W1H 1DT
Tel: 0171 724 7672
*Simple, space-saving furniture systems and accessories (Also available MO).*

**SPACE**
214 Westbourne Grove
London W11 2RH
Tel: 0171 229 6533
*Furniture and unusual pieces
by new designers.*

**TWENTIETH CENTURY
DESIGN**
274 Upper Street
London N1 2UA
Tel: 0171 288 1996
*Modern-design furniture and
lighting. (Also available MO)*

**VIADUCT FURNITURE LTD**
1–10 Summers Street
London EC1R 5BD
Tel: 0171 278 8456
*Contemporary pieces, including Refolo
computer table.*

# KITCHENS

**BELLING APPLIANCES**
Talbot Road
Mexborough
South Yorks S64 8AJ
Tel: 01709 579902
*Full range of cookers, including compact cooker.*

**DIVERTIMENTI**
46–7 Wigmore Street
London W1H 9LE
Tel: 0171 935 0689
*Wide selection of kitchen equipment.
(Also available MO on 0171 386 9911)*

**C.P. HART & SONS LTD**
Newnham Terrace
Hercules Road
London SE1 7DR
Tel: 0171 902 1000
*Modern kitchen and bathroom furniture, and
accessories. (MO)*

**THE KITCHENWARE COMPANY**
36 Hill Street
Richmond
Surrey TW9 1TW
Tel: 0181 948 7785
*Kitchen utensils, cutlery, china, and glassware.*

**LAKELAND PLASTICS LTD**
Alexandra Buildings
Windermere
Cumbria LA23 1BQ
Tel: 015394 88100
*Wide range of kitchenware and storage.
(Also available MO)*

**MERLONI DOMESTIC
APPLIANCES**
Merloni House
3 Cowley Business Park
High Street
Cowley
Uxbridge
Middx UB8 2AD
Tel: 01895 858200
*Wide range of appliances,
includings slimline cookers.*

**THE SOURCE**
26–40 Kensington
High Street
London W8 4PF
Tel: 0171 937 2626
*Modern and classic kitchenware, storage,
bathroom accessories, and lighting. (Also available
MO on 01703 336141)*

**TEFAL UK LTD**
11–49 Station Road
Langley
Slough
Berks SL3 8DR
Tel: 01753 713000
*Kitchenware, including non-stick contact grill.*

**WHIRLPOOL UK LTD**
PO Box 45
209 Purley Way
Croydon
Surrey CR9 4RY
Tel: 0181 649 5000
*Range of domestic appliances includes slimline
washing machines.*

# BATHROOMS AND HEATING

**ANTIQUE BATHS OF IVYBRIDGE LTD**
Erme Bridge Works
Ermington Road
Ivybridge
Devon PL21 9DE
Tel: 01752 698250
*Reproduction and original
sanitaryware including sitz bath.*

**BISQUE LTD**
244 Belsize Road
London NW6 4BT
Tel: 0171 328 2225
*Modern radiators and heated
towel rails. (Also available MO)*

**FLO RAD HEATING**
Unit 1, Horseshoe Business Park
Lye Lane
Rickett Wood
Herts AL2 3T
Tel: 001923 893025
*Suppliers of Thermoboard underfloor
heating system.*

**C.P. HART & SONS LTD**
See listing under Kitchens.

**KALDEWEI**
PO Box 18
Kettering
Northants NN14 1LS
Tel: 01933 405244
*Shower trays and bath tubs, including
corner baths.*

**RUNTALRAD LTD**
Airport Service Road
Portsmouth
Hants PO3 5PD
Tel: 01705 654536
*Bespoke radiators.*

**SHOWERLUX**
Sibtree Road
Coventry
W. Midlands CV3 4EL
Tel: 01203 639400
*Baths, shower trays and enclosures, including
Piccolo and Maddalena systems for tight spaces.*

**SIMPLY BATHROOMS**
Unit 2, Felnex Trading Estate
190 London Road
Hackbridge, Surrey SM6 7EL
Tel: 0181 773 5009 for details
*Space-saving Combiswing swivelling basin. (MO)*

**W. & G. SISSONS LTD**
Carrwood Road
Sheepbridge Industrial
Estate
Chesterfield
Derbys S41 9QB
Telephone 01246 450255
*High-tech steel sanitaryware.*

**VASCO PLC**
Units 14–16
Bradfield Road
Finedon Road Industrial
Estate
Wellingborough
Northants NN8 4HB
Tel: 01933 278802
*Range of modern radiators and
heated towel rail.*

**VITRA (UK) LTD**
121 Milton Park
Abingdon
Oxon OX14 4SA
Tel: 01235 820400
*Ceramic tiles and sanitaryware, including the Studio Spacemaker and the Studio Showerbath.*

**VOLA UK LTD**
Unit 12, Ampthill Business Park
Station Road
Ampthill
Beds MK45 2QW
Tel: 01525 841155
*Jacobsen range of bathroom fittings.*

**ZEHNDER LTD**
Invincible Road
Farnborough
Hants GU14 7QU
Tel: 01252 515151
*Designer radiators.*

## SLEEPING

**THE FUTON COMPANY**
Tel: 0171 221 2032 for details of your local branches.

**FUTON EXPRESS**
23–7 Pancras Road
London NW1 2QB
Tel: 0171 833 3945
*Futons and metal beds. (Also available MO)*

**YAKAMOTO FUTON COMPANY**
339B Finchley Road
London NW3
Tel: 0171 794 8085
*Futons and bean bags. (Also available MO)*

## HOME OFFICE

**BISLEY OFFICE FURNITURE**
FC Brown (Steel Equipment) Ltd
Queens Road, Bisley
Surrey GU24 9BJ
Tel: 01483 474577
*Office furniture, filing units, and accessories.*

**CASTLE GIBSON**
106A Upper Street
Islington
London N1 1QN
Tel: 0171 704 0927
*Secondhand, traditional office furniture including filing cabinets.*

**VIADUCT FURNITURE LTD**
See listing under Furniture & Accessories.

## LIGHTING

**LONDON LIGHTING COMPANY**
135 Fulham Road
London SW3 2RT
Tel: 0171 589 3612
*Modern domestic lighting.*

**LUXO UK LTD**
4 Barmeston Road
London SE6 3BN
Tel: 0181 698 7238
*Flexible general and office lighting.*

**NICE HOUSE**
See listing under Furniture & Accessories.

**THE SOURCE**
See listing under Kitchens.

## FLOORING, MATERIALS AND COMPONENTS

**ABET LTD**
70 Roding Road
London E6 4LS
Tel: 0171 473 6910
*Decorative laminates for furniture, surfaces, and floors.*

**AMTICO**
The Amtico Showroom
18 Hanover Square
London W1R 9BD
Tel: 0171 629 6258
*Wide choice of flooring materials.*

**BROADAKER CO LTD**
Church Road
St Sampsons
Guernsey, Channel Islands GY2 4LW
Tel: 01481 46818
*Manufacturers of Pivotelli brackets for televisions and speakers. (Also available MO)*

**CRUCIAL TRADING LTD**
79 Westbourne Park Road
London W2
Tel: 0171 221 9000
*Wide range of natural fibre floor coverings. (Also available MO)*

**DLW FLOORING LTD**
Centurion Court
Milton Park
Abingdon
Oxon OX14 4RY
Tel: 01235 831296
*Range of flooring including linoleum, wood, PVC, and cushioned vinyl.*

**FELS-WERKE**
8 Trinity Place
Midland Drive
Sutton Coldfield
Warwickshire B72 1TX
Tel: 0121 321 1155
*Fermacell gypsum fibreboard for walls and flooring.*

**FIRST FLOOR**
174 Wandsworth Bridge Road
London SW6 2UQ
Tel: 0171 736 1123
*Extensive range of flooring, including vinyl, rubber, wood, and carpet.*

**HÄFELE (UK) LTD**
Swift Valley Industrial Estate
Rugby
Warwickshire CV21 1RD
Tel: 01788 542020
*Components for pull-out beds, storage units, carousels. Trade only.*

**LUXCRETE**
Premier House
Disraeli Road
Harlesden
London NW10 7BT
Tel: 0181 965 7292
*Wide range of glass blocks.*

**JAMES HAMILTON ASSOCIATES**
Unit 265, Riverside Business Centre
Haldane Place
London SW18 4LZ
Tel: 0181 870 6668
*Specialist plaster finishes.*

**THE HARDWOOD FLOORING CO.**
146–52 West End Lane
London NW6 1SD
Tel: 0171 328 8481

*Reclaimed and new wood flooring.*

**JUNCKERS**
Wheaton Court
Commercial Centre
Wheaton Road, Witham
Essex CM8 3UJ
Tel: 01376 517512
*Natural wood flooring, including beech and ash.*

**KEE KLAMP LTD**
10 Worton Drive,
Worton Grange
Reading
Berks RG2 OTQ
Tel: 0118 931 1022
*Scaffolding system for building platforms, ladders.*

## LOFT CENTRE PRODUCTS
Quarry Lane Industrial Estate
Chichester
W. Sussex PO19 2NY
Tel: 01243 785246
*Loft ladders, space-saving stairs, and spiral staircases, adjustable on site.*

## MADE OF WASTE
Tel: 0171 278 6971
*Multicoloured recycled plastics sheet.*

## W.H. NEWSON & SONS LTD
61 Pimlico Road
London SW1W 8NF
Tel: 0171 978 5000
*Building materials including pegboards and clear PVC.*

## NU-LINE BUILDERS MERCHANTS
315 Westbourne Park Road
London W11 1EF
Tel: 0171 727 7748
*Architectural and general ironmongery, plumbing supplies, paint, and timber.*

## PLASTICS EXTRUDERS
Russell Gardens
Wickford, Essex SS11 8DN
Tel: 01268 735231
*Tensional strapping safety flooring.*

## H.C. SLINGSBY PLC
Unit 8, Delta Park
Smugglers Way
London SW18 1EG
Tel: 0181 877 0778
*Industrial trolleys, storage, shelving, flooring, components. (Also available MO)*

## STORAGE

## AFTER NOAH
See listing under Furniture & Accessories.

## COLOUR BLUE
See listing under Furniture & Accessories.

## THE CUBESTORE
38 Grosvenor Road
London W4 4EG
Telephone 0181 994 6016
*CubeKit modular storage system. (MO)*

## THE HOLDING COMPANY
243–45 Kings Road
London SW3 5EL
Tel: 0171 352 1600
*Wide range of space-saving storage and suspended wardrobe sytstems. (Also available MO)*

## KEY INDUSTRIAL EQUIPMENT LTD
Blackmoor Road
Ebblake Industrial Estate
Verwood, Dorset BH31 6AT
Tel: 01202 825311
*Wide range of industrial crates and shelving.*

## OCEAN HOME SHOPPING LTD
Freepost LON 811
London SW8 4BR
Tel: 0800 132985.
*Modern storage, lamps, and home accessories. (MO: 24-hour delivery)*

## PAPERCHASE
213 Tottenham Court Road
London W1P 9AF
Tel: 0171 580 8496 for details of your local branches.
*Wide range of stationery, including colourful files and storage boxes. (Also available MO)*

## SCREENS AND SHUTTERS

## THE LONDON SHUTTER CO.
18 Brockenhurst Road
Ascot, Berks SL5 9DL
Tel: 01344 28385
*Custom-made, internal cedarwood shutters.*

## SCP
135–39 Curtain Road
London EC2
Tel: 0171 739 1869
*Modern furniture, including screens and sofabeds.*

## THE SHUTTER SHOP
Queensbury House
Dilly Lane
Hartley Wintney
Hants RG27 8EQ
Tel: 01252 844575
*Hardwood louvred shutters.*

## SILENTGLISS LTD
Star Lane
Margate, Kent CT9 4EF
Tel: 01843 863571
*Blinds, curtains, dividers, including angled attic blinds.*

## ALISON WHITE
Ground Floor, Fitzpatrick
Building, York Way,
London N7 9AS
Tel: 0171 609 6127
*Solid and translucent screens, perforated blinds and lighting.*

## USEFUL ORGANIZATIONS

## THE BRITISH BATHROOM COUNCIL
Federation House
Station Road
Stoke-on-Trent
Staffs ST4 2RT
Tel: 01782 747074
*Information on all aspects of bathroom design.*

## THE BRITISH CERAMIC TILE COUNCIL
Station Road
Stoke-on-Trent
Staffs ST4 2RT
Tel: 01782 747147
*Guidance and technical advice on ceramic floor and wall tiles.*

## BUILDERS MERCHANTS FEDERATION
15 Soho Square
London W1V 6HL
Tel: 0171 439 1753
*Trade association representing builders merchants. Can provide legal and technical advice.*

## GLASS & GLAZING FEDERATION
44–48 Borough High Street
London SE1 1XB
Tel: 0171 403 7177
*Advice on specialist glazing.*

## INSTITUTE OF PLUMBERS
64 Station Lane
Hornchurch
Essex RM12 6NB
Tel: 01708 472791
*Register of recommended plumbers.*

## NATIONAL ASSOCIATION OF PLUMBING, HEATING, AND MECHANICAL SERVICES CONTRACTORS
Ensign House, Ensign Business Centre
Westwood Way
Coventry
Warwickshire CV4 8JA
Tel: 01203 470626
*Trade association of plumbers who operate a code of fair trading. Technical advice and help in contacting registered firms.*

## ROYAL INSTITUTE OF BRITISH ARCHITECTS
66 Portland Place
London W1N 4AD
Tel: 0171 580 5533
*The RIBA Client Advisory Service for recommended architects in your area.*

# INDEX

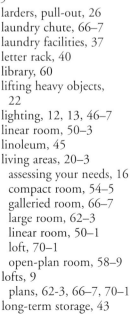

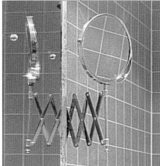

# ACKNOWLEDGMENTS

## AUTHOR'S ACKNOWLEDGMENTS

I would like to say a big thank you to everyone at Dorling Kindersley for keeping me in line to work on this book at a major turning point in my life, and in particular to Irene Lyford, my editor, for her composure, to the creative book designer Ina Stradins, to Ally Ireson for inventive picture research, and to Charlotte Davies, the series editor, for her sensitivity; not forgetting my original editor, Sally Paxton, now in distant parts, who got the project up and running.

Many thanks also to those who allowed us to invade their homes, and to the talented photographer Jake Fitzjones, whom I met by chance, and his inspired stylist partner Shani. She is so good at her job that the owner of a new studio photographed for the book bought the props that she found to decorate his flat.

A very special thanks also to Lois Love for all her leads, and especially to the architect Clifton Page for demonstrating that small spaces can be very pleasant to live in.

## PUBLISHER'S ACKNOWLEDGMENTS

Dorling Kindersley would like to thank: Ally Ireson for picture research; Robert Campbell for technical support; Hilary Bird for the index; Sharon Moore for design assistance; Sally Paxton and Murdo Culver for their work on the early stages of the project; Sacha Talbot-Dunn at Warner's Film & Location Transport for help with furniture transport; Jim Thompson for help with a lighting crisis.

We would like to thank the architects whose plans appear in the book: Andrew Hanson and Nazar al-Sayigh of Circus Architects 66–7; Jason Cooper Architect 58–9; Seth Stein Architects 70–1; Simon Colebrook of the Douglas Stephen Partnership 62–3; Voon Yee Wong of VX Designs 54–5.

We are also grateful to Guy Greenfield Architects (7, 24–5tc, 34bl) and Clifton Page Architect (22c) for help with other locations.

We are indebted to the following people who generously allowed us to photograph in their homes: Cheryl Bell, Jake and Shani Fitzjones, Rt. Hon. Nicholas Gage, Ian Hay, John Howells, Natalia Inclan, John Knights and Lesley Craig, Sue Macartney-Snape, Clifton Page, Voon Yee Wong.

We would also like to thank the following individuals and companies who lent us photographs and items for photography: Abet Ltd; Aero 14tl, 22–3c; 23tc, 26br, 41c; Helen Allen 4br, 16tl, 22bl, 86t; Alouette Innovation Ltd 21cl, 83b; Antique Baths of Ivybridge 33tl; Arc Linea 16bc, 25bc; Ariston 85b; Alouette Innovation Ltd 21cl, 83b; Tomoko Azumi 21bl, 21bc, 21br, 35tr, 85t; Cheryl Bell 47bl; Belling Appliances Ltd 25tr; James Bermudez 1, 30bl, 30bc, 34tr, 34–5c, 35tl, 82b, 88bl; Bisque 9r; But Furniture 40cl; Campbell and Young 45tr; Cato 40bc; China & Co 44br; Crabtree Kitchens 26bl; Crucial Trading Ltd; Dimplex 86; Divertimenti; Elizabethan Photographic/Abet Limited 6tl; Susan Fairminer 46–7; Jonathan Field 38cl; 38–9bc; First Floor 44tr, 45tl, tc, bl, br; Fitzroy's Flower Workshop Ltd; Robert Fleming Designs; Futon Company 20bc, 20br; Graham & Green; Habitat 3cl, 23br, 29br, 31tc, 46tr, 46tr, 46br, 47tl, 47tc, 47tr, 84b; Thomas Hall 21c, 21cr; Ian Hay 47bc; Heal's; The Holding Company 40br, 41tc; Simon Horn 35br; Ikea 10br, 15tl, 17br, 23tl, 35cr, 41bc; Innovations 41tr; Key Industrial 31cr; The Kitchenware Company; John Knights 8bl, 8cl; Manhattan Loft Corporation 8tc; Meyer 24bl; Muji 20cr; Paperchase 31bc; Pivotelli 23cr; Poggenpohl 26bc, 27tr, 27br, 28bl, 36bc; Precious McBane 12l; Primrose & Primrose; Radiant Distribution 47br; Rainbow Carpets & Curtains Ltd 45bc; Rembrandt Arts & Crafts; The Rug Warehouse; Scotts of Stow 24cl, 25cr; SCP; Winfried Scheuer-Authentics 88tr; Simply Bathrooms 17tl, 33cr; John Strand 24bc; Strouds of London; N.V. Vasco 10cr; Tefal 37ct; Tenco 32bc; Viaduct 4bl, 11r; 15bl, 29tr, 31cl, 83t; Vola UK Ltd 81cr; Whirlpool 37tr; Alison White 5br, 11tl, 87t, front jacket main image; Zanussi Ltd 25br, 27tc.

Thanks also to Tim Head for permission to photograph his work of art "Levity", 47bc.

## ARTWORK

David Ashby 22tr, 25bl, 31bc, 43bc. Richard Lee 3, 5cl, 5bl, 50c, 50–1c, 54c, 54–5c, 58tl, 58c, 62c, 62–3c, 66c, 66–7c, 70c, 70–71c, 77 (scale plans), 78–79 (floor plans), 80–81 (plans and elevations).

## PHOTOGRAPHY

All photography by Jake Fitzjones, Andy Crawford, and Matthew Ward except: Peter Anderson 27cr, 27bc, 28tr, 76–77 (measuring your room); Avotakka/Camera Press 52tr; Richard Bryant/Arcaid (architect: Pierre D'Avoine) 73; Jeremy Cockayne/Arcaid (architect: Yann Weymouth) 72tl; Peter Cook/View (designer: Hugo Tugman Partnership) 57; Friedheim-Thomas/Elizabeth Whiting & Associates 60tl; Chris Gascoigne/View (designer: Nick Hockley at Orms) 65, 72bc; Steve Gorton (front jacket main image); Graham Henderson/Elizabeth Whiting & Associates (designer: Sue Pitman) 60bl; Rodney Hyett/Elizabeth Whiting & Associates 52tl; Ray Main 44cl, 60–1, 69; Diana Miller 26tr; Nadia Mackenzie/Elizabeth Whiting & Associates 68bl; Ian Parry/Abode 68–9; Alberto Piovano/Arcaid (architect: Kris Mys) 72bl; Spike Powell/Elizabeth Whiting & Associates 13br; Roger Ressmeyer/© Corbis 6bl; Trevor Richards/Abode 60tc; Paul Ryan/International Interiors (designer: Miki Astori) 52br; Paul Ryan/International Interiors (designer: John Michael Ekeblad) 64tr; Ianthe Ruthven 46l; Paul Ryan/International Interiors (designer: Kristina Ratia) 56tl; Fritz von der Schulenburg/The Interior Archive 41tl; Fritz von der Schulenburg/The Interior Archive (designer: Dot Spikings of Bare Foot Elegance) 53; Andreas v. Einsledel/Elizabeth Whiting & Associates 68tl; Schöner Wohnen/Camera Press 20tr, 38tr, 38cr; C Scott Frances/Esto (Corrine Calesso, Architect) 52bl; C Scott Frances/Esto (Walter Chatham, Architect) 42bl; C Scott Frances/Esto (Thomas Leeser, Architect) 64bl; Elizabeth Whiting & Associates 39br; Elizabeth Whiting & Associates 56bl, 56c; Elizabeth Whiting & Associates 64tl.

Every effort has been made to trace the copyright holders. We apologise for any unintentional omission and would be pleased to insert these in subsequent editions.

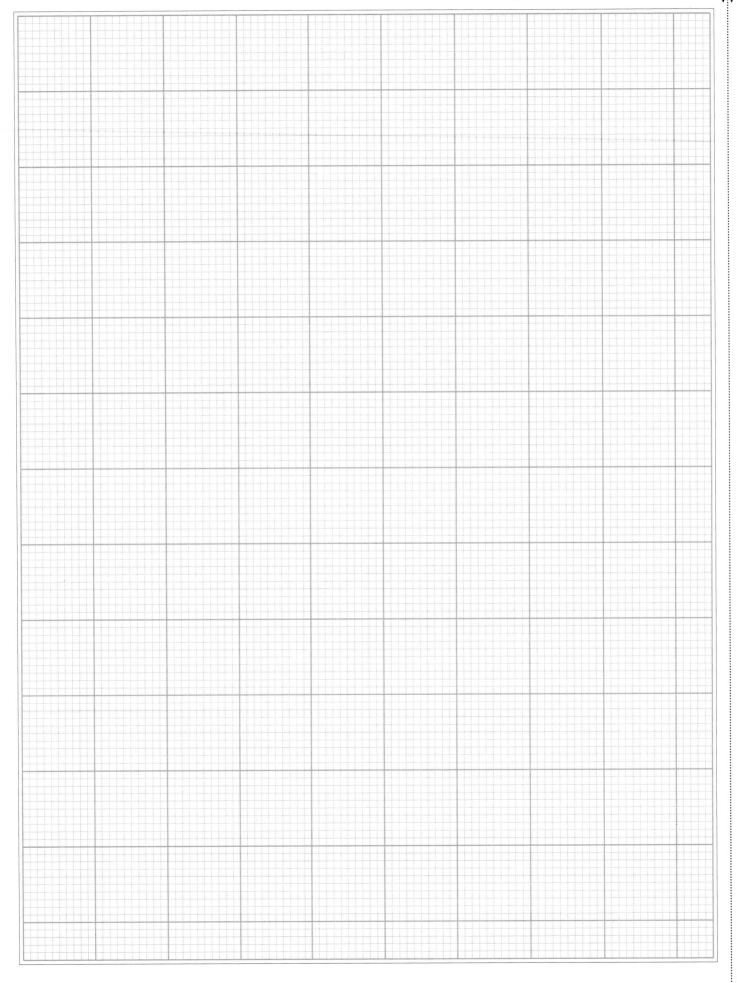

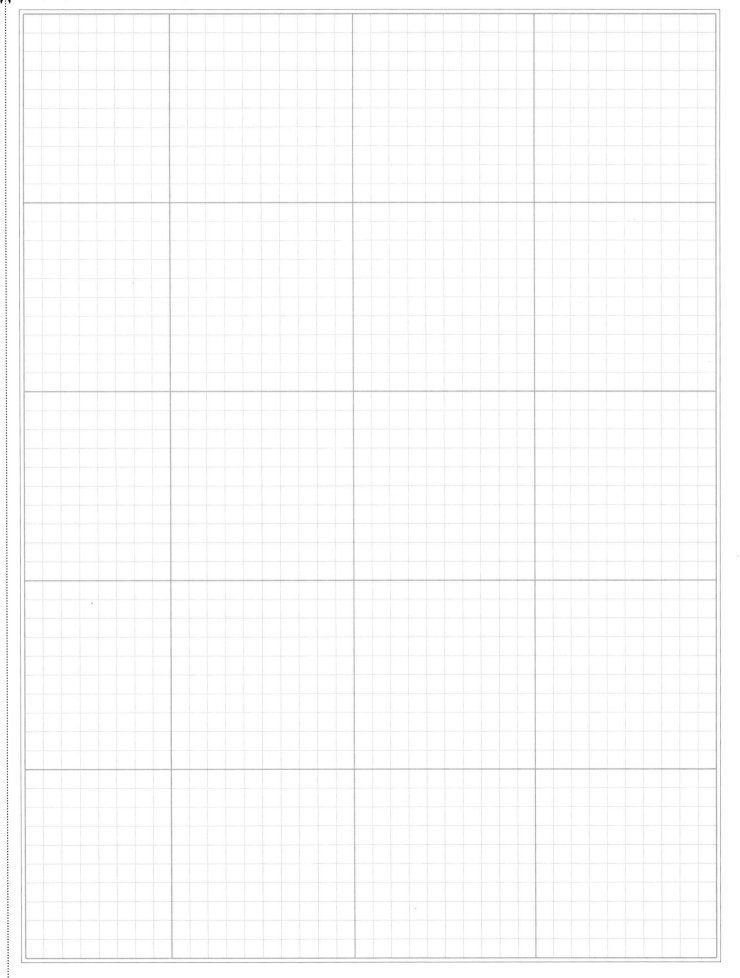

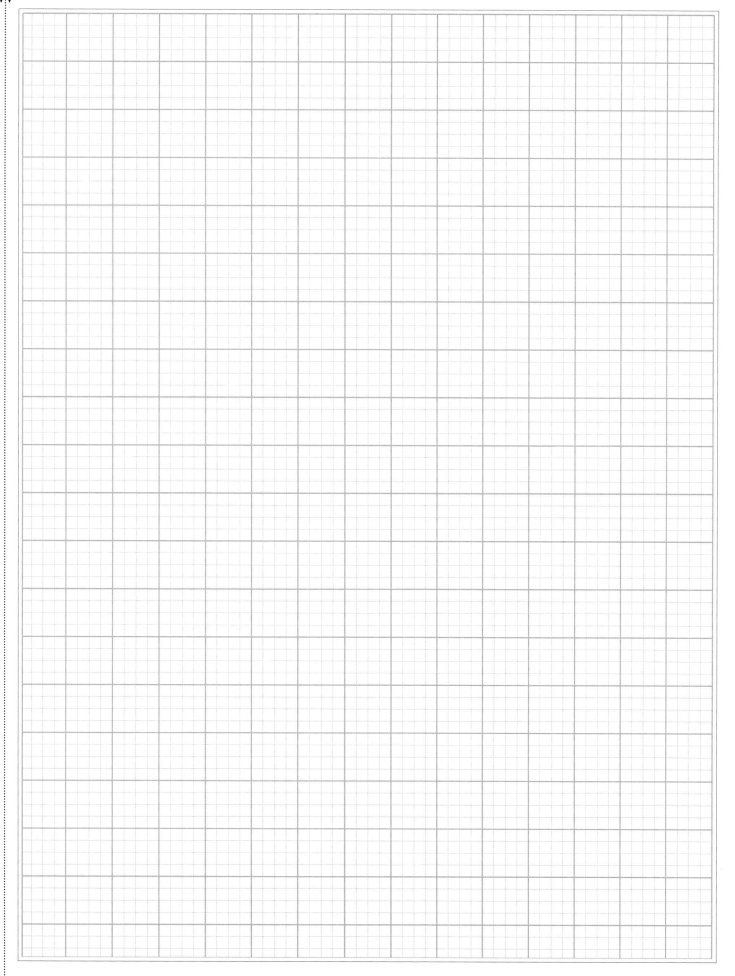

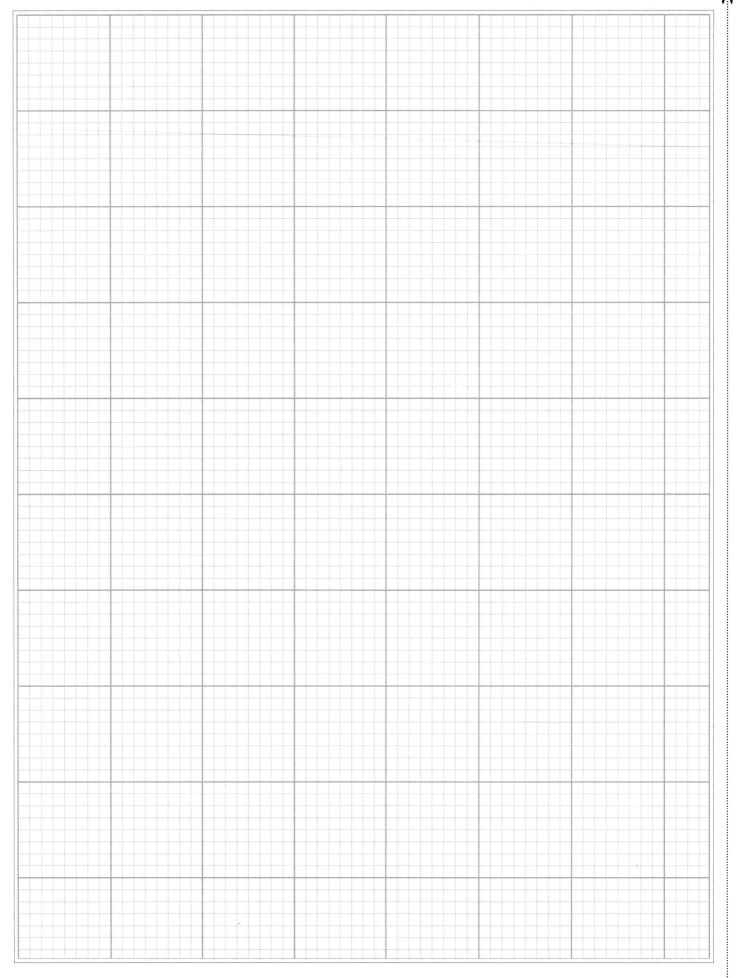

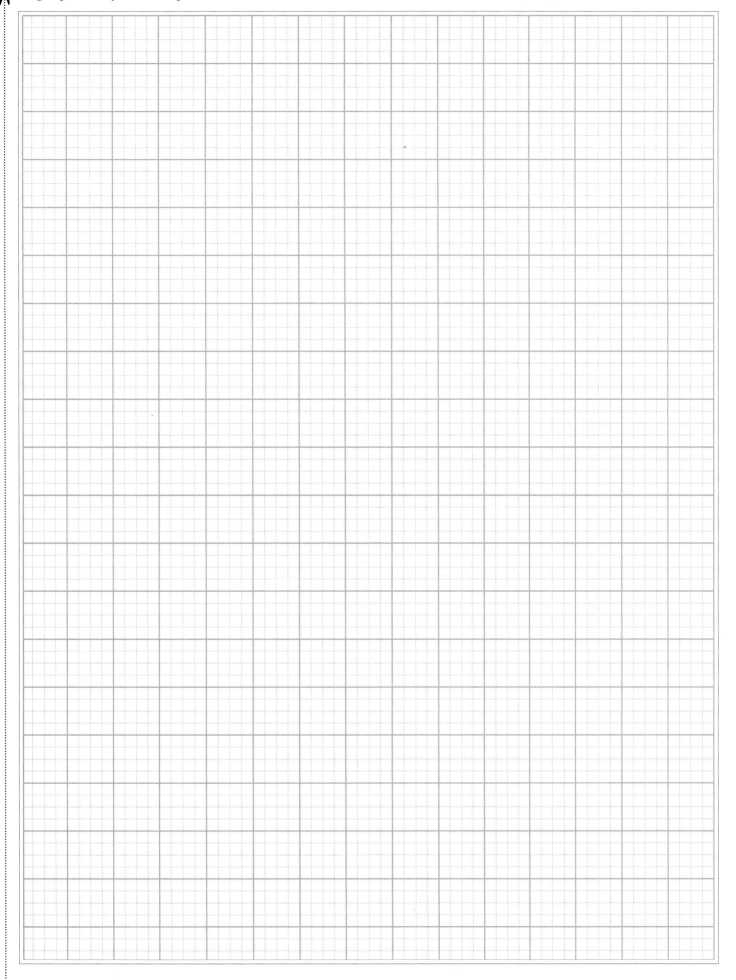

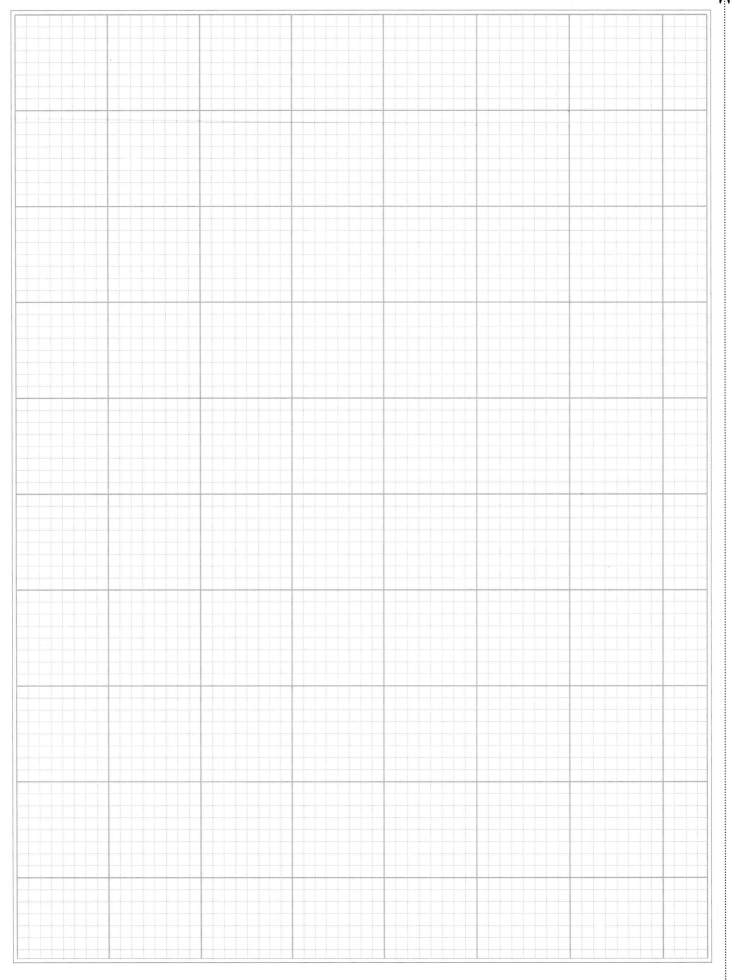